the Single Woman's Guide *to* Real Estate

All You Need to: Buy Your First Home • Buy a Vacation Home
Keep a Home After a Divorce • Invest in Property

the Single Woman's Guide *to* Real Estate

Donna Raskin and Susan Hawthorne

Adams Media
Avon, Massachusetts

This book is dedicated to my mom, Bev Pagano, who has always taken good care of herself and her children, in all ways, including financial, and who was a strong and independent woman long before it was fashionable.—Donna Raskin

To all the great customers I have worked with for over twenty-three years and to my family for understanding that I absolutely HAD to take that phone call during dinner—AGAIN!—Susan Hawthorne

Published by Adams Media, an F+W Publications Company
57 Littlefield Street, Avon, MA 02322 U.S.A.
www.adamsmedia.com

ISBN: 1-59337-552-2
Printed in The United States of America.
J I H G F E D C B A

Library of Congress Cataloging-in-Publication Data
Raskin, Donna.
The single woman's guide to real estate : all you need to buy your first home, buy a vacation home, keep a home after a divorce, invest in property / Donna Raskin and Susan Hawthorne.
p.   cm.
ISBN 1-59337-552-2
1. Real estate investment--United States. 2. Women in real estate--United States. 3. House buying--United States. 4. Single women--United States--Economic conditions. I. Hawthorne, Susan, II. Title.

HD259.R37 2006
643'.12086520973--dc22

2005034592

This publication is designed to provide accurate and authoritative information with regard to the subject matter covered. It is sold with the understanding that the publisher is not engaged in rendering legal, accounting, or other professional advice. If legal advice or other expert assistance is required, the services of a competent professional person should be sought.
—From a *Declaration of Principles* jointly adopted by a Committee of the American Bar Association and a Committee of Publishers and Associations

Many of the designations used by manufacturers and sellers to distinguish their products are claimed as trademarks. Where those designations appear in this book and Adams Media was aware of a trademark claim, the designations have been printed with initial capital letters.

This book is available at quantity discounts for bulk purchases.
For information, call 1-800-872-5627.

contents

Chapter 2: The People You'll Meet 77

Chapter 3: The Process and the Paperwork 93

part 2: Specific Situations and Scenarios

acknowledgments

First and foremost we would like to thank and formally acknowledge Paula Munier, a true friend who also happens to be our editor. Paula is a great single woman—warm, funny, kind, loving, and supportive—and she bought a house by a lake on her own. Thank you, too, to J. Scott Gannon, with The New York Mortgage Company, LLC, and Katherine McNally with Carlson GMAC for their help with mortgage information. Finally, thank you to all of the women who shared their stories. We enjoyed each conversation and appreciate your advice and wisdom very much.

Introduction

Why Single Women Are Buying Homes in Droves

Every woman—whether she is single or part of a couple—makes the decision to buy a house for her own personal reasons. The decision could be based on financial reasoning or emotional longing or a combination of both. Whatever the reason, there are important steps that everyone must take in order to choose the right house, as well as the right mortgage, insurance, and other things that go along with this major purchase.

The decision to buy a home is both more difficult and, at the same time, easier as a single woman. The difficulty can be emotional ("Will I be alone forever if I buy this house?") or financial ("I only have one income. What if I lose my job?").

On the other hand, the decision can be easier because you're single. You can choose the house you want. (Maybe you'll choose a condo so you don't have to do lawn work or worry about outdoor repairs.) You don't have to worry about someone else's credit score or financial reliability. It's good for a woman to know that she can stand on her own two feet.

But even though you're a single woman, it's important to remember that some of the issues you will deal with through the home-buying process are universal—even couples and single men have the concerns and irritations you'll have with all the paperwork and negotiating. Married people and single men worry about money and commitment; they worry about location and taxes just like you will. Buying a home is a big decision for any person, no matter what romantic or familial situation they are in.

Nevertheless, we believe that single women are a special enough group and have enough specific concerns to warrant their own book. Because, as the famous author Virginia Woolf once wrote, "A woman must have money and a room of her own if she is to write." She mentioned writing because literature was her particular dream, and she mentioned only one room because, in her day and age, women weren't legally allowed to own property. Any home a woman lived in, in fact, anything she wore, ate, used, and read, belonged to a man—either her husband, father, or even a brother or uncle.

So, the most significant point for you to remember is that no matter what your dream: to be a singer or a gardener or take care of children, you too need to find a way to provide a home for yourself. You need to have your own space and money, you should not hope that someone will gift these things to you or wait around until that happens.

But you should also know that the majority of women will one day marry and share their finances and their home with a man. We aren't telling you to take care of yourself and buy a home because you are going to be alone forever. We just believe that even if one day you share your house and life and finances with a significant other, your relationship will be that much stronger if you are confident and secure about your own financial abilities.

Of course, there are other, more fun reasons to buy your own home: you can paint it however you like, put nails wherever you like, knock down a wall, or add a room. You can get a dog, have five cats, or put in a fireplace. You can grow a backyard of daisies or put in a pool.

Likewise, you don't have to rely on a landlord to fix any problems that arise. If something is leaking, you can take care of it. If you want a repair made, you can handle it right away. Many renters have problems with landlords snooping, being overly intrusive, or being unreliable and unhelpful. If you own the house, you can take care of it to your own satisfaction.

The house is yours and you will have a feeling of ownership that gives many women a sense of security and "home" in a way that nothing else can.

It's Also about Money

Aside from the psychological and emotional benefits, there is another very important reason to buy a house on your own—it makes good financial sense. The U.S. government allows taxpayers to deduct a portion of a home loan's interest from their annual taxes. This is significant, because home loans (a.k.a. mortgages) are set up such that the interest is paid off first, so that the first few years after you buy a home you can deduct a large portion of your mortgage payments from your annual taxes, which is an enormous savings for most people.

While it's true that you have to wait until April 15th to see the money, it is a significant chunk of cash to get. And, in fact, you can actually deduct the amount you expect to get back from your paycheck if you want. In other words, you can choose to increase the deductions you claim on your taxes so that you don't have to wait until April to see that money again.

But that's not the only financial reason to buy a home. Everyone has to pay for the place they live in one way or another. If you live in an apartment, you pay rent; if you live in a house that you've bought, you pay a mortgage. However, the rent goes into your landlord's pocket and you get no tax break and, at the same time, you aren't building equity. Equity means value, because if you put your rent money toward a mortgage, you are actually paying that money back into your own pocket in the long run, because you own a little bit more of your home with each and every mortgage payment you make.

Let us explain more clearly: Let's say you take out a $300,000 mortgage. Your first month's payment is $1,500, and almost all of that payment is interest. The bank actually owns the home and the land it's on, while you own a very small percentage based on that tiny payment you made. As time goes on, though, your payments make a larger and larger dent into that $300,000 (and the interest the bank is charging). This way, over the course of the loan, you become the full owner of a home, which usually by then is worth well more than what you paid for it.

Therefore, unlike someone who just paid rent all those years, you now own something worth perhaps $500,000 (depending on the how housing prices have increased).

When Renting or Living with Your Family Is Best

Now, this doesn't mean everyone should go out and buy a house immediately. There are times when renting on your own or living with your family is best, both psychologically and financially.

In the first place, if you know you aren't going to be in an area longer than one to three years, then it's possible that the costs associated with buying and selling real estate might eat up the profits you would typically see in home appreciation even with the tax break figured in. While some areas, such as big cities, have house prices that rise demonstrably very quickly and so even in two years, you might see a financial gain from buying; other areas, such as the South, often don't have big swings in housing values. Also, in some places, homes don't sell quickly, which means you could end up holding onto a house even after you've moved away from that town.

Another time it might be better to rent or live at home is if you have a lot of credit card debt or don't really have enough money to pay a mortgage (or to put down a down payment that will help you have a reasonable mortgage). With the rising costs of houses, many women are buying homes that are a lot more expensive than what they can comfortably purchase. But mortgage lenders and banks are now more likely to offer money—and larger sums of it—to more people, because they do, in the end, reap the benefits of those loans (in the form of larger and larger interest payments from more consumers).

In some ways, this situation can be likened to an exclusive department store offering you a credit card to buy a pair of shoes that you can't afford to pay for with cash. Here's what we mean: Let's say you could buy a pair of black pumps for $85, but you also see a nicer pair for $300. You don't have $300, so the department store offers you a credit card (with interest, of course) so you can buy them. You end up paying $352 for the shoes (after interest) when, in fact, the $85 pair would have made you just as happy.

Now, there are times when stretching your financial limits a bit is a good thing because, in the end, it might pay off. But there is a fine line between financial stretching and financial stress. Real financial stress—where you can't pay your bills or worry about how you're going to make it until your next paycheck—is a horrible thing to experience. Financial stress will keep you up at night and make you irritable and not necessarily bring you any financial rewards in the end. So, in general, it's better to avoid a situation that will put you under serious financial strain.

How to ease the stress over the decision to stay at home or buy

Talking to yourself about the positive and negative points about whether you should buy or stay at home (or rent) is just as important as learning about mortgages and looking for a house. These are some of the issues you should contemplate. And don't worry if your decision is to stay at home for a while—a good financial decision isn't just one that comes to the conclusion of purchasing. The only right answer is one that has been arrived at through responsible consideration.

- Be prepared for unexpected expenses and potential problems. Don't overbuy. In other words, just figure that you are getting your feet wet by buying a small condo or house and then, in five years, you can move up to a house that is more ideal.
- Talk to your parents about whether they would rather you live at home to save for a down payment or whether they would prefer to lend you the down payment and have you get your own place. It's possible that they will help you make a decision that everyone is comfortable with.
- Don't make the decision using just your gut, get the hard facts. Create a table and figure out how much it will cost you to (a) rent for five years, (b) live at home for five years

(to save for a down payment), or (c) buy a small place. Then, looking at those facts, ask yourself which situation would benefit you most. See "Should I Rent? Live at Home? Or Buy?" on page 214 for a sample table.

Remember, there is no right answer. There may be a right financial answer, but money is not always the most important aspect of a problem or situation.

If your finances are a problem, whether because of debt or low pay, don't pull strings or move heaven and earth just to get a mortgage. There are smarter things to do in this situation. First, try to fix your financial problems. Pay off some debt, take on a second job to increase your income (or get a better job), or save some money by living with your family so you can make a larger down payment.

Here's another idea: Live for a few months as if you are paying a mortgage. For example, let's say your rent is $950, and your mortgage would be $1,500. Pay your rent and put $550 in the bank (or, if you have to, give it to someone else to hold onto). See how that feels to your psyche and your pocketbook. If doing this doesn't create a lot of stress, then you are probably ready to buy your home (plus you have some more money saved up!).

There are two more scenarios in which it's probably best to rent (or live with your family) rather than buy a home: First, if your relationship with your co-buyer, be it friend, boyfriend, or family member, is problematic. Houses are not problem solvers. In fact, arguing about money will make anyone sad or angry, or make an unfortunate situation worse. Now, we realize you are a single woman buying a home, but perhaps you are thinking your boyfriend is going to move in with you or that your mother (who drives you crazy) can cosign the loan on the house you want. We encourage you to not assume that buying a house will fix or improve any relationship. It won't. Instead, wait to purchase until you can do so without added stress or aggravation because of another person.

Finally, there is one more reason to not buy: if you don't have the time or inclination to take care of a property by yourself. You won't necessarily have to mow the lawn or re-pave the driveway, because perhaps you'll buy a condo, and so someone else will do those things, but if you are in school or work a lot or just don't like sleeping in a house by yourself, listen to those concerns. Don't ignore them. Talk to a friend or family member about your concerns. Whether it's landscaping or loneliness, ignoring these things and blindly forcing yourself to go through the home-buying process isn't as important as your peace of mind. Plus, if you talk about your worries, you might be able to find a solution that will both reassure you and allow you to gain financial equity.

Buying a home can be one of the best things you will ever do for yourself, but it's not the solution to every problem or the secret to happiness. We encourage you to take on this responsibility only when it is clearly and surely the right financial and life step for you.

Some perspective

As a woman, you will:

- Live longer than most men.
- Earn less than most men.
- Be out of the work place for a few years due to child rearing.
- Have less in savings when you retire.

Buying a home is a good investment even if you get married because your financial life is your own (not your husband's), and it is absolutely intertwined with your longer life span and child-rearing choices in a way that his won't be. Even a woman who is married has to accept the reality that her financial life will be different than her husband's because she will live longer and, even if she works, will most likely take time off from her career for child rearing, so at the end of her working life, her pension, social security payments, and savings will be different from her husband's.

Psychological Blocks

For women, home buying is not just a financial situation, it's a psychological one. Weird questions will pop into your mind—questions that aren't quite appropriate for your real estate agent (should you really tell her your boyfriend woes?) but that, at the same time, aren't quite intense enough to put you on the couch.

Let's just make a blanket statement—buying a house won't and can't affect your future relationship status. No "rules" book has ever come out and said, "Don't take care of yourself because, if you do, no one will come along and rescue you." Even Cinderella, Snow White, and the Pretty Woman had to work and find places to live; in fact, part of what made them so lovable and appealing was their abilities to take care of themselves.

The truth is, the better you take care of yourself—in every way— the better you'll take care of yourself when it comes to relationships. When women feel afraid and unable to care for themselves, they are more likely to stay in unhealthy relationships. If you are strong enough to support yourself and give yourself shelter then you won't compromise your feelings or physical safety in order to make sure you (and perhaps your kids) have food and a place to live. At the same time, you'll be better able to choose a partner who will also be responsible and capable.

On the other hand, perhaps you are worried that you won't be able to take care of a house by yourself. We know a woman who desperately wanted to buy a house, but she had a cat that liked to bring home "presents" of the dead and furry variety. This woman, strong and capable as she was, couldn't bring herself to dispose of the critters herself and always appreciated her landlord doing it for her. "If I live alone in a house, I'll have to scrape the little buggers off the driveway myself," feared Ms. Not Afraid of Anything Else in the World. Could she tell a real estate agent this? Would anyone be able to solve this problem for her? No. What ended up happening? Well, she did eventually buy a house herself (and it was lovely: three bedrooms, a fireplace, one acre) and yes, her cat did bring home a dead chipmunk one day. Ms. Not Afraid of Anything Else in the World actually went next door and asked the man of that house to take care of the problem. Which he kindly did. She returned the favor with a bottle of wine.

Or perhaps you actually fear for your life and safety. Many women are afraid that someone will break into their house in the middle of the night and rape or kill them. (Sorry to be blunt, but we believe in being honest about our fears.) This fear can be resolved with knowledge and common sense.

First, your safety is much more dependent on whom you live with and who your neighbors are than whether or not you live alone. There is a difference between domestic violence and random violence, and domestic violence is much more likely than random. If you live in a safe neighborhood and you don't live with an abusive boyfriend, husband, or relative then, statistically speaking, you live a safe life. But the key words there are "safe neighborhood." Don't buy a nice home in a bad neighborhood, because not only will you feel nervous and possibly be in danger, but also the odds are good that your home won't be worth much in the end anyway.

No matter where you live, you should do all you can to protect yourself, especially if safety is your number-one concern: Get alarms, make sure your windows and doors are secure, make sure your outside area is well-lit, and consider changing the locks on the doors when you move in. Remember: Living alone as a woman is a risk, but it's not as risky as driving drunk or being in an abusive relationship.

Finally, there is also the fear of getting ripped off: Because you are a woman, it is likely that real estate agents (even female ones), contractors, inspectors, and mortgage lenders will bring their prejudices and opinions to the table. You might not be treated as fairly or respectfully as you would like. Trust your instincts and ask questions. If you sense someone isn't answering you honestly or is talking down to you because you are a woman, then trust your opinion. You always have the right to talk to someone else about the information you are getting and your concerns. Another good tactic is to bring this book or information printed out from the Web with you when you meet with lenders so that you can point to your research to back up your claim or question.

In this day and age, many real estate agents are used to—and enjoy—working specifically with women. But, in case you are confronted with someone who doesn't, don't allow your "disease to please," i.e., your fear of standing up for yourself, to get in the way of getting the home you want at a price that is appropriate. If someone isn't willing to give you the level of respect you deserve, find someone else who will.

The home-buying process is almost always stressful. Studies have, in fact, shown that most people agree: All of the steps and details in the process are confusing and discouraging. Buyers start with a dream— three bedrooms, lots of light, and a spacious backyard—only to come face-to-face with what's available on the market, how much they can afford, and the piles of paperwork and confusing terms. This sense of being overwhelmed happens to all homebuyers, but it can be especially frustrating to the first-time homebuyer who is going through the steps on her own.

In fact, realestate.com conducted a study which found that the home-buying process is very much like a roller coaster, where the buyer feels "high" when they find a house or make an offer, and "low" when they are waiting for approvals and offer acceptance. The highs and lows then continue in a predictable pattern, following when the buyer is in control (high) and when she is waiting for someone else to make a decision (low). None of this is surprising, of course.

But throughout the process, an overwhelming number—more than 60 percent—said that being patient was the best thing they could do to make each step less stressful.

The survey also found that 41 percent of the buyers used the Internet to research houses, school districts, real estate agents, and mortgage rates. And here's some fun info: Overwhelmingly, the thing most people wanted for their first night in their new homes was window coverings—that far and away beat out the 8 percent who wanted to drink champagne!

How to Use This Book

As we said, no matter whether you are single or married or a woman or a man, the home-buying process is, financially speaking, the same for everyone. Every buyer has to find money for a down payment (or borrow it), get a mortgage, figure out the taxes, and get insurance. So, much of the information in this book isn't strictly regarding being a woman.

However, we believe that women need their own book for two reasons. First, because, as women ourselves, we believe we have a fun, intimate way of communicating even the driest, most mundane information. So, we think you'll actually enjoy reading our book even while you're learning everything you need to know about mortgages and home buying.

Second, we think single women do have a few concerns that are special to their situations, and most home-buying books do not address these questions. A woman's safety, a concern for her children, the desire for a beautiful home as well as a functional home are topics you don't see in most mortgage 101–type books.

Therefore, we designed this book to be comprehensive, fun-to-read, and reassuring. We want you to feel comfortable no matter what your situation and to know that you are not alone. Other women have been in your shoes and they have succeeded in buying the homes of their dreams.

Of course, we realize that you aren't a single woman buying your first home, a vacation home, and a retirement home at the same time. This book is written for all single women, though, no matter what your age or home-buying interest. So, we advise you to start with the chapter on your particular situation to get a sense of what your specific concerns and questions might be. Then, move onto the first few chapters that have financial, credit, and other home-purchasing advice that pertains to every buyer.

Finally, we hope you'll read the chapters (they aren't too long) with advice for other women. One of the things we learned as we wrote this book is that women have a lot to teach each other and that it's amazing how many women go through this process on their own. They all have interesting, reassuring, financially lucrative, and inspiring stories to tell.

Women have, traditionally, been the people in families who decorate, clean, and care for houses. To be sexist for a moment, we believe that it is women—and their children if they have them—who make a house a home. So isn't it about time that women claim their purchasing power and actually own the homes they nurture?

Dealing with All the Paperwork

As soon as you walk onto the front steps of a home that is for sale, a real estate agent (yours or the seller's or even both) will hand you a stack of papers. These usually include a page or two with a picture of the house and a detailed list of its rooms and amenities. The agent may also give you a seller's disclosure sheet, which gives information on the condition of the home and often includes comments by an inspector. It's also mandatory that the real estate agency disclose to you whom the broker represents, the buyer or the seller.

At the same time, the agent will hand you her business card and, possibly, a list of other homes that might fit what she thinks you are looking for. These are called "comps," and they can be used to show why the house is priced as it is and also to show you other homes you might want to see (so the real estate agent can retain your business if this isn't the home you want).

Then, later, you will speak to mortgage lenders, inspectors, and maybe builders or repairpersons. In the end, you will be bombarded with numbers, facts, opinions, and official offers and data from a minimum of five people. Plus, you will also have to keep track of your own numbers, facts, and opinions.

With all of this information, the more organized you are, the better you'll be able to make clear decisions. We have left room in this book for you to write in the tables and forms in Part 3, but you may need to do the same calculations and lists with anywhere from two to twenty homes.

So, our suggestion is that you get a notebook with folders in it, or a binder with room for papers and folders, so that you can write down the name of every person you speak to, as well as keep track of the information they give you. If someone gives you financial information or important details about a house (such as how old the oil tank is or how much the average electric bill is) you'll want to make sure you can refer back to that information when necessary.

Go to open houses in your area before you contact a broker to familiarize yourself with the market. Find out prices and ask the real estate agent at the house about other properties. You might meet your perfect broker match at an open house.

Meanwhile, begin to jot down your thoughts and impressions of the houses you see. You might spend an afternoon looking at a bunch of homes and, at the end of the day, it will be difficult to remember which one has the blue bathroom that needs repainting and which one has the rickety stairs leading into the basement.

These points aren't just personal preference ideas, either. You will be able to use each of these considerations when you begin to formulate your offer and negotiate the deal.

Be sure to bring this book with you, too, as you talk to people. We don't expect you to quote verbatim from it or to necessarily refer to it while you're sitting in front of a loan officer, but we can tell you that if you walk into a lender's or real estate agent's office with a reference book they will immediately know you have done your homework. This will, we believe, make it clear that they should be up-front and clear with you, answering your questions and not making the assumption that you don't understand what they're talking about.

On a separate note, throughout the home-buying process, you should also have a place to keep any receipts related to your search, including photocopying of forms and information, because you want to make sure you have a complete record in case any issues should later arise.

The Ten-Step Home-Buying Process

1. Get preapproved to see roughly how much you can spend for a home.

2. Look for the house you want to buy.

3. Make an offer on the house.

4. When your offer is accepted, get a home inspection.

5. Go back to the lender and apply for the loan.

6. Sign the purchase and sale agreement.

7. Get the loan and commitment from the lender.

8. Do the title work.

9. Go to closing.

10. Move in!

Linda's Story:

"I take good care of myself financially."

Linda Martin, 42, Robbinsville, NJ

I was thirty-one and living with a roommate who was getting married, so I had to make a decision about whether I should find a new roommate, which I really didn't want to do. I was looking at places to rent alone, but I wasn't making a huge amount of money at the time. My sisters suggested I live with my mom for a year and then buy a place. I really didn't want to move back home, but it allowed me to save money for a down payment on a house, which, in turn, would allow me to build some equity. I had been working two jobs and I realized that the one job was really just paying taxes. I didn't have children or another tax write-off. Buying property was a smart thing to do because suddenly I could get some write-offs and itemize when I did my taxes.

So, economically it made a lot of sense, and personally it made a lot of sense. I was really ready to have my own place. I could finally really unpack and put nails in the walls.

I was making $32,000 a year back then, and I was also bartending one or two nights a week, but I wouldn't let them take my bartending money into consideration when they prequalified me, even though I continued bartending a couple of years after I bought the house. Once you buy a place, you don't end up paying the mortgage you think you're going to pay, you always pay more. I was determined to keep my mortgage under $700 a month, so I wanted the lender to do her calculations on my salary, rather than my entire income. This would insure that I wouldn't end up borrowing more than I was comfortable paying.

In fact, the advice I would give any person looking to buy is not to overextend. You're going to want to furnish the place. You want to make sure you can afford it; and you need to know that your taxes will go up. Don't let some real estate agent or your big eyes influence your

(continued)

decision. You see these beautiful homes and you walk into them and there's no furniture. And allow some room for things that you don't expect to happen.

Safety is also huge to me. I would rather live in a hut in a really nice neighborhood than in a big house in an unsafe area. I can run here and not always look over my shoulder. I know my neighbors, and they know me. As a single woman, I'm thrilled they notice who's going in and out of my place.

Taking Pride in What I Did

I had read an article about women who didn't purchase property because they were waiting to get married. But, to be honest, I didn't think I was giving up. I was quite proud of myself that I had bought something and it was a phenomenal investment. And, at the time I didn't know it would be so beneficial.

I bought a condo and everyone advised me against it. Everyone told me I would lose money. But I couldn't afford to buy a house, and I didn't want the huge responsibility of a house. I don't have to shovel my walk. If my roof goes someone else will fix it.

In fact, at the time, an appraiser friend of mine basically said to me, "It's not a great investment but if you want to own something at least you'll own something." So, I bought it for $72,500, and now it's up to $200,000. It turned out to be one of the best decisions I made in my life.

Of course, the monthly fees have changed over these ten years. In fact, over the last two years they've risen from $103 a month to $135 a month. But, in the meantime, I'm the manager of a marketing department for a public records firm, and about a year-and-a-half ago I got a very nice raise. So, I started to look for townhomes in this area. I started shopping around and I saw a couple of units that I liked and that I thought I might be able to afford. But then my father died and we had to pay for his funeral. The expenses freaked me out, and I haven't gone back to looking.

I take good care of myself financially because no one would take care of me if something happened. I do have that in the back of my mind. I have to take care of myself, and I don't have a safety net.

I have to make sure I make my bills. I don't have credit card bills. I have money saved and a 401(k).

But, I don't want somebody taking care of me. I don't think that a man is going to come into my life and save me. I don't need to be saved. I think that the belief in someone saving you ends up driving a lot of women to compromise. I don't have to compromise. I try not to overextend myself. I'm basically a very responsible person anyway. I'm a very structured person. My big addiction in life is exercise. ❦

part 1

The Nuts and Bolts
for Any Buyer

Chapter 1

All about Mortgages

"Where should I live?" and "How much house can I afford?" These two questions—or variations on the theme ("Can I afford that colonial on Oak Street?" "Should I live near my parents or across town?" "Should I move across the country?")—are the first and most basic questions everyone asks about buying a home. A home purchase—actually, any property purchase, whether it's for you to live in, to invest in, or for you to vacation or retire in—is all about money and location.

Just because these are the first two and the most basic questions doesn't mean they are unimportant or easy to answer. While some of us will suddenly see the perfect home and fall in love fast and quickly without asking these questions, most of us will need to think through our answers in order to make a decision that helps us feel secure and certain. In fact, these decisions are, to use a home metaphor, the foundation on which the rest of your decisions will rest.

So, first, we are going to discuss the money, which, in terms of houses, means mortgages. The word *mortgage* translates from Latin to "pay until death"—it's a large loan and it takes a long time to repay it. We want you to see an example of the variation of numbers you will get when you look at different types of mortgages:

Type	Rate	APR	Monthly P&I Payment	One Fee Closing Cost
30-year-fixed	5.750%	5.916%	$1,097.12	$2,899.42
15-year-fixed	5.375%	5.657%	$1,523.67	$2,992.85
5/1 interest-only ARM (LIBOR Index)	5.375%	6.139%	$842.08	$2,655.58
5/1 ARM (LIBOR Index)	5.250%	6.097%	$1,038.14	$2,833.80
3/1 ARM (LIBOR Index)	5.000%	6.188%	$1,009.22	$2,819.52

Mortgage Basics

As we said, no matter what type of property you are buying—your first home, a vacation house, a retirement place, or an investment property—there aren't clearly defined mortgage loans geared to different types of property. There are differences between types of mortgages, but what type of home you use them for is up to you. Some mortgages are designed specifically for particular types of buyers, such as first-time homeowners, but that doesn't mean you have to take out a loan by that name, nor does it mean it's your only borrowing option.

Now, when most people use the term *mortgage*, they are referring to the monthly payment they make toward owning their home. But, in reality, the payment comprises not just the principal and interest on the loan, but what lenders more properly call a **PITI** payment. Each letter stands for one portion of the four costs, which are combined into one payment to make check-writing easier. They are:

P **Principal.** The loan balance; the actual amount of money you borrowed. If your house costs $300,000 and you have $10,000, you'll want to borrow $290,000.

I **Interest.** The interest owed on the principal. This is how much your lender is charging you for the loan.

T **Taxes.** Taxes assessed by different government agencies to pay for school construction, fire department service, etc.

I **Insurance.** Coverage against theft, fire, hurricanes, and other disasters. If you put down less than 20 percent, you'll actually have to insure the loan, too.

You have the last word on how much you want to borrow, not the lender (although they have the last word on what you *can* borrow). In other words, just because they say you can afford to pay $2,500 each month, is that how you want to spend your money? Or do you want something left over each month for shoes or a vacation fund? It's your money and you need to know how much will make you happy to spend.

Because buying a house is such an important aspect of financial independence in our capitalist system, the government and various financial institutions have come up with diverse plans that allow all types of people to buy a home of their own. This is good news, because it means that people in all kinds of economic situations can become homeowners.

Terms to know

A **mortgage** is a long-term loan that a borrower obtains from a bank, credit union, independent mortgage broker, online lender, or property seller. The house and the land it sits on serve as the **collateral** for the loan. The borrower signs documents at the closing that give the lender a **lien** against the property. A lien gives the lender the power to take the home through **foreclosure** if the borrower doesn't make payments as agreed.

But this also means that you have a choice in how to borrow money, and with choice comes the importance of research. You need to understand the specifics of each type of loan so that you know which one will work best for you.

The differences between the loans involve interest rates, down payments, and payment schedules. The loan you are offered and its terms will be determined by how much cash you have, your credit rating, and your income.

In order to understand the different types of loans, you need to fully understand each term used to define and differentiate the types of loans, such as interest, points, and so on. We're going to explain each term and loan very specifically when we discuss each one, but we want to give you a glossary of words and terms right away. It will probably take you a little bit of practice and study of various terms before you feel confident that you understand the various mortgages that are available, but we want to assure you that the more you understand the more likely you are to get the right loan.

All The Terms You're Going to Hear

Abstract of title—A summary of events, dates, and recordings regarding a specific property title. (See also Title.)

Accrued interest—Earned interest that hasn't yet been paid. For example, if a loan is designed with accrued interest then that money is paid when it reaches maturity. Interest builds throughout the loan's term and is paid as a lump sum on the date the loan is due in full. When you make a mortgage payment, you are actually paying the interest from the previous month. It's the exact opposite of paying rent, which is paid on the date when money is due for the following month.

Acquisition cost—All of the fees associated with the purchase of a property.

Acre—Unit of measurement used to buy land. One acre is equal to 43,560 square feet of land.

Addendum—A document or piece of information added to legal documents. An addendum becomes part of the contract and is as legally viable as all other parts of the contract.

Adjustable-rate mortgage (ARM)—A type of mortgage loan that allows the interest rate to change at specific intervals, which are agreed upon on signing for a determined amount of time.

Agent—Someone who acts on behalf of someone else in exchange for a fee.

Amenities—This term is used during an inspection, and it refers to benefits related to a property that don't necessarily have a specified monetary value, such as a view or attractive architectural touches, i.e., crown molding.

Amortization—A payment installment plan; repaying a debt over time in periodic installments.

Amortization schedule—The debt repayment schedule. It identifies the specific payment amounts and dates, including which part of the payment goes to principal and which part goes to interest. The payment schedule usually also includes the unpaid balance so you can see how much is left on the loan at any given time.

Annual debt service—The total amount (principal and interest) required for the loan, although you pay a monthly debt service.

Annual percentage rate (APR)—The effective rate of interest charged over the year for a loan.

Apartment—A residential dwelling contained in a multifamily building, usually rented to a tenant.

Appraisal—The estimated value of a property. Because some property values change so quickly, it is sometimes difficult to get this number to line up with the price you're paying for a property. An appraiser comes up with this number and cannot have a vested interest in the property.

Appurtenance—An item outside the property but considered a part of the realty.

"As is" agreement—When a property is sold without warranty or guarantee, whatever condition it is in at the time of agreement. Everyone involved in a sale like this must understand local laws surrounding this term.

Asking price—The listed sale price of a property. Many owners assume offer prices will be lower than the asking price, although in very competitive housing markets asking prices are just starting figures, and sellers get offers higher than the asking price.

Assumption—When a buyer takes over the loan payments and debt from a seller. Both the buyer and the seller are then responsible for repayment if someone defaults on the loan. Sometimes called assumable mortgage.

Attachment—When a property is seized to force payment of a debt.

Balloon payment—A lump sum of money due at a specific time. Balloon mortgages include payments like these written into the loans.

Broker—Someone with a license, granted by the state, to act on behalf of others (for a fee) in a real estate deal.

Building codes—Rules and regulations adopted by local governments for a minimum level of consistency in building practices.

Building permit—A license from a local government to build in a specific place.

Chain of title—The history of a property's title.

Clear title—A property that has no mortgages or liens associated with it, so it can be sold immediately.

Close/Closing—The procedure and the time when a seller transfers a property to a buyer.

Closing costs—Fees incurred during the closing of a real estate transaction. These can include commissions, discount points, and legal fees.

Closing statement—A piece of paper(s) detailing the full accounting of all sources, fees, and uses of funds in a real estate transaction.

Collateral—Property or goods pledged to secure a loan.

Condominium—An individual property connected to common areas that are co-owned and operated by the other individual property owners.

Contingency—A provision stating that a contract isn't viable until a certain act or agreement has been completed.

Contingency contract—A contract that has a contingency within it.

Cooperative (co-op)—A property that allows the owner to also have stock or ownership in the company that owns the property, as well as use of that property. You own shares of a stock rather than having a deed to a property.

Co-owners—Two or more people who have equal legal responsibility and rights for a property.

Cosigner—A person who signs and assumes joint liability for a loan with another person.

Counteroffer—A rebuttal to an offer. Offers and counteroffers can go through a series of negotiations and conditions.

Creative financing—Financing plans or loans that are different from traditional 30-year fixed-rate loans.

Credit report—A financial history from independent organizations that attempts to define a person's reliability and financial responsibility. These reports are notorious for having errors, so you should be aware of what's in your credit history at all times.

Curtailment—A payment made ahead of schedule that shortens or ends a mortgage.

Damages—Compensation paid or offered to make up for loss or injury caused by an illegal act or negligence.

Deed—A legal document that transfers a real estate title from one person or group to another.

Deposit—Money offered to the seller from the buyer to guarantee that the buyer's contract requests will be fulfilled. Sometimes called "earnest money."

Discount points—Fees paid to the lender at the time of the loan origination to offset the difference between the note rate of the loan and the true percentage rate.

Down payment—Money that is not part of a loan paid as equity and security toward the purchase of a home.

Duplex—A residential property with two residential dwellings within it.

Dwelling—A place of residence within a residential property.

Earnest money—Money given with a purchase offer to guarantee good faith and performance of the contract.

Easement—The right, license, or privilege to use someone else's property.

Encroachment—An intrusion or obstruction on someone's property.

Entitlement—A legal right of an individual, usually associated with VA loans.

Equity—The cash value of a property minus all liens against it.

Escrow—Money, used as a sign of trust or agreement, held for one party by another.

Fair market value—The price of a property at a particular time in a specific market (area, location).

First mortgage—A mortgage with priority over other mortgages.

Fixtures—Items in the house that are attached to the property's sale, but not necessarily an unmovable part of the house, like the refrigerator, chandeliers, or the stove.

Gifted money—When someone gives money without any expectation of repayment. This can be used as a down payment. People who give a gift for a home down payment should always check into the tax laws regarding their gift.

Income-to-debt ratio—A formula used by lenders to determine how much money a borrower can comfortably pay. The traditional ratio has always been 28 percent, meaning 28 percent of your total monthly income can be used to pay the total amount comprising principal, interest, taxes, and insurance.

Inspection—An examination to determine the quality of property.

Interest-only loan—A loan with terms requiring only the payment of interest at regular intervals until the loan reaches maturity.

Interest rates—The percentage of a loan a lender charges the borrower for a specific amount of money.

Leverage—Borrowing money to increase the amount of your potential investment

Lien—A financial claim against a property. Liens may include mortgages, loans, trusts, overdue property taxes, unpaid bills, condo fees, and utility bills. Titles searches are done to make sure there aren't unacknowledged liens against a property.

Line of credit—When a lender agrees to offer a specific amount of money without further loan applications.

Loan origination fee—A fee charged by lenders for the processing of the loan. It's often equal to one percent of the loan.

Loan-to-value ratio—A formula used by lenders to determine how much they should lend in relation to a property's worth. They usually want to have a property worth $100 for every $80 they lend.

Locking in—Mortgage rates fluctuate wildly and, in the past, borrowers have found themselves with a different rate at signing than they were quoted when they first spoke to the lender. To counteract this problem, borrowers pay a fee to "lock in" a rate they have been quoted.

Mortgage banker—Someone who originates, sells, and services mortgage loans.

Mortgage broker—Someone who arranges mortgage financing for a fee.

Multiple Listing Servce (MLS)—A real estate listing service that assigns numbers to keep track of properties on the market. You'll see an MLS# when you search on real estate agent.com or another real estate Web site.

Net income—The amount of money remaining after all expenses are paid.

Net worth—The amount of equity left after all liabilities are subtracted from assets.

Offer—A proposal that, if it is accepted, becomes a contract. For properties, buyers typically make written offers to sellers. The seller can then accept, reject, or counter the offer. Buyers can withdraw an offer at any time before it has been accepted.

Option—The right to take an action if certain conditions are met.

Points (loan discount fee)—An interest fee charged by lenders at settlement. One point is equal to one percent of the mortgage. Points raise the lender's yield about the interest rate. The buyer or seller or both, according to the regulations of the loan (FHA, VA, etc.), may pay points.

Secondary mortgage market—When investors or companies buy mortgages from primary lenders. This is very common and it is likely that, over the life of your loan, your mortgage will be sold to other lenders.

Title—Proof of ownership of a piece of property and the buildings on it.

Mortgage Types—Their Differences and Which One Would Work Best for You

It's very important to understand the differences between the details of each type of mortgage in order to make sure you're going to spend your money in the way that is right for you. For example, you might decide it's worth it for you to write a larger check each month if it means that you'll pay less interest over the years. Or, perhaps, you prefer to write a smaller check each month so that you can have that extra money in your checking account—just in case you need it for an emergency or to spend the way you want to—even if it means paying more in interest for the loan overall.

It's important that you know there is no one right way to do this. Everyone's money personality is different, and everyone defines security and financial responsibility differently (although, of course, in general, spending more than you have is irresponsible).

If you really can't keep track of these types of details or if the numbers become overwhelming, we suggest bringing this list with you to the mortgage lender or your real estate agent and asking them to run all the number options for you, so you can see what each monthly check would look like over the years. Don't let someone dismiss one or more options based on their own opinion of what's a better type of loan. Once again—what's better for your lender or your friend or your real estate agent may not be better for you.

Second mortgages

A second mortgage is a loan that uses the equity in your home (the difference between what you owe on the home and its current value) as security. This allows you to refinance existing loans, pay off outstanding debts, or perhaps finance other significant expenses, such as medical bills. This is a second loan, so your first mortgage takes priority over all other loans negotiated using the property as collateral.

Here is a list and a general statement about each type of home loan, some of which are more traditional types of mortgages and others of which are new or unconventional ways to finance a home purchase. We'll start by giving you a general idea of all of your options before you get into the nitty-gritty of mortgages:

- **Fixed-rate loan**—This is the most common loan. You pay a set (fixed) amount of money for a set (fixed) amount of time, such as 15, 20, or, most commonly, 30 years. You pay the same amount each month for the life of the loan. You can usually pay extra toward the principal without penalty, which means you can pay off the loan sooner than you are supposed to. This is the most basic kind of loan, so it's not as "new" or "sexy" as other options a mortgage lender will tell you about, but it's very important that you ask about this option, because as you advance in your career, or if you end up with a second income, you may be able to increase your payments each month and thereby pay off your mortgage sooner without having to pay all of the interest amortized into the loan.

- **Adjustable-rate mortgage**—In this type of loan, which is sometimes called an ARM, the initial interest rate is set when you sign the papers, but it fluctuates over the life of the loan, based on the economy's interest rate. There is a cap on how much the amount can rise over the life of the loan. In other words, your payment amount changes over time. Borrowers usually choose this type of loan because they get a very low interest rate at the beginning of the loan—and this is particularly attractive when interest rates are very high. (You get a lower rate at first, and you're betting that the general interest rate won't go higher.) Sometimes you can get a convertible ARM that allows you to switch to a fixed-term mortgage rate. This way, if interest rates go down you can set your payment at the low point.

- **Buy down**—When you're young or if you don't have a lot of money to use right away toward your mortgage, but yet, at the same time, think you will have more money available eventually, you can consider a buy down option, which allows you to start your payments off at a lower-than-average interest rate. Then, however, the rates begin to climb to a predetermined interest rate. (In other words, when you sign the loan, you'll know in advance what interest rate you're going to be paying and how much each payment will be.) What does the lender get in return? At the end of the loan, the borrower has to pay a predetermined amount of money in a lump sum to make up for the money not spent in the early days of the loan. So, you'll be paying the same sum over time, but the majority of it will be at the end of the loan, not at the beginning.

- **Assumable mortgage**—This is when the borrower takes over the current owner's mortgage, so the borrower doesn't have to take out a loan of her own. This isn't very common these days (because newer loans often now have lower interest rates), but it's always an option.

- **Construction mortgage**—These loans are designed to help you borrow the money to build your home, as well as purchase the land. It enables you to not have to take out another loan once the house is built.

- **Interest-only mortgage**—A loan in which all of the payment goes toward the interest and none toward the principal. We'll discuss this type of loan in great detail later in the chapter, as it's very popular these days, and a woman who takes out this type of loan needs to be very sure this is what will work for her over time.

- **Jumbo mortgage**—"Jumbo" refers to the amount (or size) of the loan. These days, any loan from $359,650 to $750,000 is a jumbo, while loans from $750,000 to $1 million are super-jumbo. But these numbers change from year to year, as housing prices change. Jumbo and super-jumbo loans usually have higher interest rates with additional fees, although people with hefty bank accounts can work out these mortgages with their banks to try to avoid these fees.

- **Seller financing**—This is when the seller provides the mortgage loan to the buyer, so the seller becomes the lender.
- **Rent to own/lease with option to buy**—The buyer moves into the home, paying rent to the seller, who then applies a percentage of that money to a future down payment on the home. The buyer usually gives a small down payment to the owner as a show of good faith.
- **Two-step mortgage**—These mortgages begin as fixed-rate loans and then convert, after five or seven years, to convertible or nonconvertible ARM loans.
- **Biweekly mortgages**—With this mortgage, you make two payments each month, rather than one, which, over the course of a year, means two extra payments a year. This cuts down on the overall interest you pay over the life of the loan. Some lenders charge extra for this. Sometimes it's better to just make this extra payment on your own, rather than having the lender set it up for you. You can do this schedule with any type of loan.
- **Balloon mortgages**—This is a loan that is amortized like a traditional 30-year mortgage, but at the end of a specified period (usually five or seven years) a specific amount of the loan (a large, "balloon" amount) is due. Interest rates are lower on these loans than on traditional loans, and they can often be refinanced when the balloon payment is due (but you still have to make that payment).

How Does Amortization Work?

No matter what kind of loan you choose, the breakdown of each payment (the four amounts that go toward the principal, interest, taxes, and other fees) changes over time because mortgages are based on a repayment formula called amortization. With amortization, the lender spreads the interest you owe on the mortgage over the life of the loan.

For example, on a 30-year, $250,000 mortgage with a fixed interest rate of 6 percent, a homeowner who keeps the loan for the full term will pay $289,595 in interest—more than the amount borrowed.

The lender does not expect that person to pay all that interest in just a couple of years, so the interest is spread over the full 30-year term. That keeps the monthly payment at $1,498.88, but the majority of each month's payment goes toward interest during the early years of the loan. Of the first month's payment, for instance, only $111.32 goes toward principal. The other $937.50 goes toward interest. That ratio gradually improves over time and by the second-to-last payment, $1,484.02 of the borrower's payment will apply to principal while just $14.86 will go toward interest.

Thirty-year loans are just one way to divide up the loan payments, however. Lenders have also traditionally offered 15-year mortgages and, these days, 40-year loans.

40-Year Versus 30-Year Versus 15-Year Loans

When you don't have a lot of money to use as a down payment for a house, a 40-year or 30-year loan allows you to borrow a large amount and pay the interest on that sum without being crushed financially. The reason you are able to borrow such a large amount of money is because the entire loan amount is spread across each month of 30 years—a total of 360 payments.

The problem with this plan—for buyers at least, not for banks—is that you'll pay a huge amount of interest over 30 years. One way to fix this problem, then, is to reduce the length of your loan. The most common loan length after 30 years is 15 years. Take a look at this:

Comparison of 15- and 30-Year Loans

	30-year loan	15-year loan
Loan amount	$250,000	$250,000
Interest rate	7 percent	7 percent
Monthly payments	$1,663.26	$2,247.07
Number of total payments	360	180
Total spent over life of loan	$598,773.60	$404,472.60
The average cost of a 30-year mortgage is 48 percent higher than a 15-year mortgage.		

As you can see, by choosing a 15-year mortgage loan, you could save significant money over the cost of the loan in interest. Of course, the monthly payments are significantly different, too, which is why most people choose the 30-year option. However, we did want to show you why you should at least consider this type of loan. If you can afford the extra money each month, it might be worth the extra effort.

Also, 15-year loans are usually offered at interest rates slightly lower than 30-year mortgages, so you will also save money in that way, too. At the same time, it's often difficult to qualify for this type of financing, because lenders will need to see that you are able to make the higher monthly payments.

Prepayments

Just because you have a 30-year fixed-rate loan with a payment of $1,100 doesn't mean you can't write a larger check each month if you are able to. This is called prepayment, and the extra money is applied to your principal, which brings down the total amount of your loan. Let's say, for example, that you receive a bonus of $1,000 or a tax refund of $3,000. You could, if you wanted, send that money to your lender to apply to your loan. If you borrowed $150,000 for your mortgage and are at the very beginning of your loan process, then the majority of your monthly payment is going toward interest. So, if you send in $3,000 to be used toward the principal, then your loan amount is reduced to $147,000, and you will be able to pay off your total loan that much sooner, since the amount of interest owed will also decrease in proportion to the new loan amount. Do this often enough, and you will significantly reduce the length of your loan and the total amount of interest you will pay.

Some lenders, however, don't allow prepayments, because this reduces the amount of money they will accumulate over the years. You need to talk to your loan officer about this and make sure that there are no prepayment penalties attached to your loan. Most loans don't have prepayment penalties, but make sure you ask your lender.

Conforming and Nonconforming Loans

It used to be that people (usually men) had to "conform" to certain criteria in order to obtain a mortgage. For instance, they had to have 20 percent of the cost of the house for a down payment, they had to earn a certain income, and they had to have a certain low debt-to-income ratio in order for a lender to sign their loan. When a borrower didn't meet these criteria but still managed to get a loan, the agreement was considered "nonconforming." These days, most consumers are nonconforming. Very few borrowers have 20 percent down, and many people have more debt than they should.

The good news is that lenders are more willing to look at each individual's situation and create a loan that will work for her. In fact, nonconforming loans are more the norm these days. Nevertheless, some lenders will still refer to various loan types as conforming or nonconforming.

Adjustable-Rate Mortgages

Adjustable-rate mortgages, or ARMs, are different from fixed-rate mortgages because the interest rate and monthly payment change as general interest rates fluctuate. ARM loans have an initial fixed-rate period during which the borrower's rate doesn't change, but that is then followed by a much longer period when the interest rate changes at preset intervals.

The fluctuating rates of the ARM are tied to the performance of one of three major indexes:

- The one-year Treasury Bill
- The 11th District Cost of Funds Index (COFI)
- The London Interbank Offered Rate (LIBOR)

The benefit for borrowers is that lenders charge rates during the initial period that are generally lower than those on comparable fixed-rate mortgages. Lenders take the risk of giving you a lower initial interest rate hoping that interest rates will be higher in the future.

So how long is the initial fixed-rate period? The lender can create loans with initial fixed-rate periods that are as short as a month or as long as ten years; one year is typical. However, these days, the standard is the 5/1 ARM. With this, the fixed-rate portion lasts five years; after which the interest rate is adjusted annually.

These types of mortgages, which mix a lengthy fixed period with even lengthier adjustable periods, are called "hybrids." Other popular hybrid ARMs are the 3/1, the 7/1, and the 10/1. As their names imply, these loans have fixed rates for the first three, seven, or ten years, with the rates adjusted annually each year thereafter.

After the fixed-rate honeymoon, an ARM's rate fluctuates at the same rate as the index spelled out in the closing documents. The lender gets the index value, adds a margin calculation, and then recalculates the borrower's new rate and payment. The lender repeats and recalculates this formulation each time an adjustment date rolls around.

In other words, you can't really predict what your interest rate will end up being over time. Nevertheless, the sky's not the limit in terms of interest rates. Borrowers have some protection from extreme changes because ARMs come with caps that limit the amount the rates and payments can change over time.

There are a number of different kinds of caps. The most common are:

- **Periodic rate cap**—This limits how much the rate can change at any one time. Usually, these are annual caps, which prevent the rate from rising more than a certain number of percentage points in any given year.
- **Lifetime cap**—This limits how much the interest rate can rise over the life of the loan.
- **Payment cap**—Less common than the other types, these are only offered on some ARMs. This cap limits the amount the monthly payment can increase over the life of the loan in dollars, rather than how much the rate can change in percentage points.

If your lender offers you an ARM, you should discuss the various types of caps and ask them to show you how the payments might differ over time. Of course, the lender will be making estimates about payment amounts, because no one can predict with 100 percent certainty what interest rates will be in the future.

Interest-Only ARMs

In these deals, the borrower pays only the interest (rather than the interest and the principal) on the loan for a fairly long time, such as ten years, then the loan adjusts to the going interest rate of a specified index. The loan then amortizes at an accelerated rate.

During the early half of the twentieth century, most home loans were interest-only. When the Great Depression hit, however, foreclosures occurred at an alarming rate because homeowners couldn't afford the payments. So began the era of the 30-year amortized mortgage, which typically required 20 percent down. Therefore, between the 1940s and the real estate boom of the early twenty-first century, lenders in this country only offered interest-only options to real estate investors and their wealthy customers. These interest-only loans were usually a type of ARM.

Now, however, with rising house prices and fewer borrowers able to pay these enormous mortgages (most of which would qualify as super-jumbo loans), lenders have begun to market interest-only mortgages to middle-class borrowers. Even though the borrower is paying only interest during the beginning of the loan, she can pay some principal, too, if she wants, usually without penalty.

On the flip side, as home prices climb, many buyers are turning to interest-only loans to reduce mortgage payments and gain more financial freedom. For example, on a 30-year mortgage with a 5-year interest-only ARM, the borrowers would pay no principal for the first five years. For the remaining twenty-five years, they would have significantly higher payments, compensating for the first five years. Interest-only options are also commonly offered for a 10/1 ARM or for a monthly adjustable rate. With a 10/1 ARM, the interest rate is fixed for ten years, and then adjusted every year thereafter.

The biggest upside to an interest-only loan is the smaller payments. The downside is that homeowners build equity only by appreciation, because they aren't paying down the principal. Because they are depending solely on appreciation, a homeowner can end up without much equity if housing prices don't rise as expected or, as is happening right now, house prices are already high and don't have much room to grow. If the market shifts and you have to sell your house for less than you paid for it, an interest-only loan gives you no equity, and you will owe the bank the difference in the two house prices—which is worse than renting in terms of what you're left with. Even if there has been some price appreciation, selling costs such as real estate commissions could wipe out any profit.

It is this situation that worries financial planners, because, in reality, these people couldn't really afford the house they are living in if it weren't for the interest-only loan.

Unfortunately, in the end, interest-only loans are an enormously high risk for traditional borrowers. If a homeowner actually has a lot of money in her pocket, then an interest-only loan is a good investment. There are no prepayment penalties on interest-only loans, so homeowners always have the option of paying down the principal. Having other savings or investments available would help absorb the shock if a homeowner had to sell at a loss. If someone can afford the house anyway, but thinks she can invest the money at a higher return than the home would bring over time, then an interest-only loan might work for her.

In addition to the wealthy, lenders recommend interest-only loans to people in three other categories:

- People whose income will jump significantly in a defined period of time, such as medical students, law students, or those opening their own business with a secure guarantee of income.
- People who are confident their home will appreciate significantly over time. This means you have to buy your house in an undervalued market. Unfortunately, many of the people getting interest-only loans now are signing on to them because the market is inflated, not undervalued.
- People who are sure they will stay in their home only for a short period of time, specifically the time period during which their loan is at a lower interest-only rate and, at the same time, they are sure their house price won't depreciate, so that (a) they will move before the interest-only period is up, (b) they wouldn't pay down much principal anyway, and (c) they know they will sell their home for the same price or higher than they bought it.

Of course, some interest-only ARMs come with a conversion feature that allows borrowers to convert their loans to fixed-rate mortgages for a fee. The popularity of interest-only loans also reflects the realization among many buyers that they will never actually own their homes outright.

Nevertheless, don't agree to stretch your mortgage out to the limit to buy a more expensive home. Homeowners often intend to save or invest money that would have gone to principal but then end up using that money for other things, which negates the purpose of taking out the interest-only loan in the first place.

Which is the better mortgage option for you: fixed or adjustable?

The low initial cost of adjustable-rate mortgages (ARMs) can be very tempting to homebuyers, but they are riskier and more uncertain loans than fixed rates, which offer rate and payment security. And no one can predict with certainty which loan will be more expensive in the long run.

Here are some pros and cons of ARMs and fixed-rate loans:

ARM pros:

- ARMs feature lower rates and payments early on in the loan term. Because lenders can use the lower payment when qualifying borrowers, people can buy larger homes than they otherwise could buy.
- 85 percent of ARMs are paid off within five years because of refinancing, sale of the house, or cost influx, so borrowers who choose this option usually do so for a reason.
- ARMS allow borrowers to make low-interest or interest-only payments for a portion of their loan terms to keep their payments low at the beginning of the home-buying time, when money is probably tightest.
- Borrowers might actually be able to keep their financial options open and sign a loan in which the ARM is convertible to a fixed-rate mortgage so the payments are not a big surprise.
- These loans can also be assumable, which means when you sell your home the buyer may qualify to assume your existing mortgage. This can work in your favor over time if mortgage interest rates are high when you are selling.
- ARMs allow borrowers to take advantage of falling interest rates without refinancing. Instead of having to pay a whole new set of closing costs and fees, ARM borrowers can potentially watch their rates drop if the interest rates are falling during their adjustment periods.
- ARMs help borrowers save and invest more money. Someone who has a payment that's $100 less with an ARM can save that money and earn more off it in a higher-yielding investment.
- ARMs offer a cheap way for borrowers who don't plan on living in one place for very long to buy a house.

ARM cons:

- No matter what the terms or rates are offered, ARM loans are more difficult to understand and less secure than fixed-rate loans.
- Rates and payments can rise significantly over the life of the loan. A 5 percent ARM can end up at 11 percent in just three years if rates rise sharply. There have been times—and they weren't too long ago—when interest rates were over 20 percent, which is scary and impossible to deal with financially when you've signed on for a loan at 5 percent.
- A borrower's initial low rate will adjust to a level higher than the going fixed-rate level in almost every case even if rates in the economy as a whole don't change. That's because ARMs have initial fixed rates that are set artificially low.
- The first adjustment can be a doozy because some annual caps don't apply to the initial change. Someone with an annual cap of 2 percent and a lifetime cap of 6 percent could theoretically see the rate shoot from 6 percent to 12 percent twelve months after closing if rates in the overall economy skyrocket.
- ARMs are difficult to understand. Lenders have much more flexibility when determining margins, caps, adjustment indexes, and other things, so unsophisticated borrowers can easily get confused or trapped by shady mortgage companies.
- On certain ARMs, called negative amortization loans, borrowers can end up owing more money than they did at closing. That's because the payments on these loans are set so low (to make the loans even more affordable) they only cover part of the interest due. Any additional amount due gets rolled into the principal balance.

Fixed-rate mortgage pros:

- Rates and payments remain constant. There won't be any surprises even if inflation surges out of control and mortgage rates head to 20 percent.
- Stability makes budgeting easier. People can manage their money with more certainty because their housing outlays don't change.
- They're simple to understand, so they're good for first-time buyers who wouldn't know a 7/1 ARM with 2/6 caps if it hit them over the head.

Fixed-rate mortgage cons:

- To take advantage of falling rates, fixed-rate mortgage holders have to refinance. That means a few thousand dollars in closing costs, another trip to the title company's office, and several hours spent digging up tax forms, bank statements, etc.
- Fixed-rate mortgages can be too expensive for some borrowers, especially in high-rate environments, because there is no early-on payment and rate break.
- Fixed-rate mortgages are virtually identical from lender to lender. While lenders keep many ARMs on their books, most financial institutions sell their fixed-rate mortgages

into the secondary market. As a result, ARMs can be customized for individual borrowers, while most fixed-rate mortgages can't.

All of these things should factor into your decision between a fixed-rate mortgage and an adjustable. But there are other important questions to answer when deciding which loan is better for you:

1. How long do you plan on staying in the home?

If you're only going to be living in the house a few years, it would make sense to take the lower-rate ARM, especially if you can get a reasonably priced 3/1 or 5/1. Your payment and rate will be low, and you can build up more savings for a bigger home down the road. Plus, you'll never be exposed to huge rate adjustments because you'll move before the adjustable rate period begins. Nationally, less than half the people with 30-year mortgages stay in place long enough to pay off that loan.

2. How frequently does the ARM adjust, and when is the adjustment made?

After the initial fixed period, most ARMs adjust every year on the anniversary of the mortgage. The new rate is actually set about 45 days before the anniversary, based on the specified index. But some adjust as frequently as every month. If that's too much volatility for you, go with a fixed-rate mortgage.

3. What's the interest rate environment like?

When rates are relatively high, ARMs make sense because their lower initial rates allow borrowers to still reap the benefits of homeownership. Rates could start to fall, meaning borrowers will have a decent chance of getting lower payments even if they don't refinance. When rates are relatively low, however, fixed-rate mortgages make more sense. After all, 7 percent is a great rate to borrow money at for thirty years.

4. Can you still afford your monthly payment if interest rates rise significantly?

On a $150,000, 1-year adjustable-rate mortgage with 2/6 caps, your 5.75 percent ARM could end up at 11.75 percent, with the monthly payment shooting up as well.

How Adjustable Rates Can Rise

Year of ARM	Rate	Monthly payment
First year	5.75%	$875
Second year	7.75%	$1,075
Third year	9.75%	$1,289
Fourth year	11.75%	$1,514
	(6% lifetime cap)	($639 more than first year)

Now, let's compare this worst-case ARM scenario to a fixed-rate mortgage:

Interest rate during four years	Total payments during four years
ARM: 5.75% to 11.75%	$57,036
Fixed rate: 7.75%	$51,600
Savings with fixed-rate mortgage over four years:	$5,436

In this case, the fixed-rate mortgage costs less than the worst-case ARM scenario. Experts say when fixed mortgage rates are low, they tend to be better deals than ARMs, even if you only plan to stay in the house for a few years.

Subprime Mortgages

Egregious credit problems, such as a recent foreclosure, will prevent you from getting a mortgage. But lesser credit flaws won't necessarily stop you from getting a home loan. An industry of subprime mortgage lenders has sprung up to serve the vast constituency of Americans who have credit problems.

The Federal National Mortgage Association (Fannie Mae) and the Federal Home Loan Mortgage Corporation (Freddie Mac) give lenders a grade.

Fannie Mae and Freddie Mac
Lender Report Card

A   Completely creditworthy.

A-   One small unpaid bill (less than $1,000) or no more than one late payment over six days or two payments over thirty days.

B   Up to four late payments in the past year or so.

C   Six late payments, accounts in collection. Bankruptcies or foreclosures resolved.

D   Currently running late with most payments.

- A borrowers are prime, everyone else (even the A-) are subprime.
- Get your current landlord to write a letter saying you pay on time and are reliable.

How to Assume an FHA Mortgage

Generally, subprime mortgages are for borrowers with credit scores under 620. Credit scores range from about 300 to about 900, with most consumers landing in the 600s and 700s. Someone who is habitually late in paying bills, and especially someone who falls behind on debts by 30 or 60 or 90 days or more, will suffer from a plummeting credit score. If it falls below 620, that consumer is in Subprime territory.

Few lenders will use the term subprime to describe you or your loan, because it's considered bad salesmanship. You might hear the word nonprime, or, more likely, an adjective won't be used to describe the mortgage at all.

Mortgages for people with excellent credit are somewhat of a commodity, with rates that don't vary much from lender to lender for equivalent loans. That's not the case with subprime mortgages. You might receive widely differing offers from different subprime lenders because they have different ways of weighing the risk of giving you a loan. For that reason, it's important to comparison shop when your credit score is less than 620.

Subprime loans have higher rates than equivalent prime loans. Lenders consider many factors in a process called "risk-based pricing" when they come up with mortgage rates and terms. This makes it impossible to generalize about subprime rates. They are higher, but how much higher depends on factors such as credit score, size of down payment, and what types of delinquencies the borrower has in the recent past (from a mortgage lender's standpoint, late mortgage or rent payments are worse than late credit card payments).

A subprime loan also is more likely to have a prepayment penalty, a balloon payment, or both. A prepayment penalty is a fee assessed against the borrower for paying off the loan early—either because the borrower sells the house or refinances the high-rate loan. A mortgage with a balloon payment requires the borrower to pay off the entire outstanding amount in a lump sum after a certain period has passed, often five years. If the borrower can't pay the entire amount when the balloon payment is due, she has to refinance the loan or sell the house.

Researchers contend that prepayment penalties and balloon payments are associated with higher foreclosure rates. The subprime mortgage industry contends that borrowers get lower interest rates in exchange for prepayment penalties and balloon payments, but that point is debatable.

Predatory Lenders

Subprime customers have to be on the lookout for predatory lenders who set out to cheat borrowers. There are several predatory tactics, and sometimes a lender will combine them. Some lenders soak naive borrowers with outrageous fees and sky-high interest rates. These lenders are likely to tell the borrower that her credit score is lower than it really is.

An ethical mortgage lender doesn't want to foreclose on a property, because foreclosure is a money-losing process. An ethical lender makes money by charging interest and loses money by foreclosing. A predatory lender, on the other hand, profits by repeatedly collecting closing fees, then seizing the house.

To defend yourself from predatory lenders, find out your credit score before shopping for a mortgage, and ask people whom you trust for referrals to mortgage lenders. And comparison shop by getting quotes from at least two mortgage brokers or lenders.

My mortgage lender keeps suggesting I refinance. Should I?

Another predatory tactic is to pressure a homeowner to refinance the mortgage frequently, charging high closing fees each time and rolling the closing costs into the mortgage amount. That goes hand-in-hand with another predatory tactic: issuing a loan regardless of the borrower's ability to repay it. When the borrower inevitably defaults, the predatory lender forecloses and sells the property.

My mortgage lender says I need two mortgages to get my house. Should I do that?

Sometimes, if you don't qualify for a loan that is the entire cost of your house, a lender might offer you two loans, a primary mortgage and a home equity loan or second mortgage (on top of the first loan), which will allow you to buy the house. But you will have to pay both loans back at the same time. And often the second mortgage will be an interest-only loan. Usually the first loan covers 80 percent of the cost of the house and the second one 20 percent, as if it's a second mortgage.

If a lender offers you this, study carefully the terms of both loans. Find out if there are any prepayment penalties on either loan. Ask the lender to tell you exactly what the monthly payment of each loan will be. If the second mortgage is interest-only, you should try to pay that down as quickly as possible in order to build equity.

By the way, some lenders try to help borrowers avoid paying PMI (private mortgage insurance, required if you put down less than 20 percent) even if they don't have 20 percent to put down by offering you a second-tier mortgage to make up the difference. The interest on the second loan will be higher, but it will be tax deductible, whereas PMI is not. As always, it pays to do your homework and explore as many options as you can with your lender.

The Types of Properties and Their Costs

Years ago, owning a single-family, detached home was the dream of every American family. These homes suited the most common living arrangement at the time: two adults and a few kids, plus a dog and a cat. Everyone had his or her own room, and the animals and kids had a place to run around.

But today's homebuyer is different. In fact, if she's *you*, buying this book, she might not necessarily want land for the kids to play on (who wants to mow a lawn?) or three bedrooms and a basement. Many women choose instead to buy condominiums or other types of property, which are more suited to a woman who lives alone or even with children.

Condominums

A **condominium** (or condo, for short) is officially a dwelling that is part of a larger structure. For example, a condo can be a two-bedroom flat in a Victorian-style home in San Francisco or a five-room apartment-style place in a 200-unit complex in Phoenix. No matter what it looks like, however, the condo owner buys a unit that also entitles her to an interest in the larger structure, such as the lawn, a pool, or other amenities. However, these amenities come at a price, so along with paying for the dwelling, a condo owner also has to pay an association fee. These fees can be minimal, perhaps only covering snow removal or lawn service, or they can be extensive, to pay for managing security, pools, clubhouses, and other expenses shared by all of the co-owners of the property. So, make sure you see the condo budget before making an offer. In fact, potential condo owners should interview the condo board treasurer to determine the financial health of the association before they move in.

Planned Unit Development

Similar to a condo is a **planned unit development**, or PUD. These types of structures are basically large neighborhoods with all kinds of housing within them (often complete with shopping areas). These developments, which seem to be appearing overnight in some parts of the United States, can include all types of housing options—single-family homes, condos, and apartments—all created as one integrated system. Sometimes these communities have association fees (for clubhouses) while other times, the town that welcomed the brand-new community taxes these new residents for their "impact" on the environment—charging residents for sewer, water, even schools.

If you buy in a PUD, you should ask about the associated fees with each type of housing. Sometimes, single-family homeowners won't have to pay condo fees, while, in other situations, some of the housing is designated as "affordable" meaning that costs are reduced for a specific number of residents who meet certain criteria (such as low-income or single-parent families).

Cooperative

Meanwhile, a cooperative or co-op is similar to a condo in that the owner of the residential dwelling also has ownership of the larger structure, but instead of paying toward an association, the owner gets shares in the corporation rather than a deed to her home. The co-op owner is then actually a part owner of the corporation that owns the larger structure she resides in. In many cities, for example, co-ops own entire apartment buildings, and there is a co-op board that passes rules and regulations to decide what is allowable within the property. Not only that, but co-op owners can't just sell their unit at any time and in any manner. Co-op boards must approve changes to your home, as well as whom you sell to.

Duplex

A duplex is often a smaller dwelling than a condo or co-op building, such as a single-family-style home that has two housing units in which each resident owns her own home and is responsible for the outside structure as well. Sometimes, a duplex can actually refer to a two-floor condo. This differs from a condo or co-op because if, for example, your lawn needs to be mowed, you are responsible for that. If something happens to the outside structure, you are responsible for the problem. The benefit of a duplex is that you don't have to pay condo, co-op, or association fees, and yet, at the same time, your house will be less expensive than a single-family home.

Duplexes often work well for women who want to live near a family member or friends but not in the same home with them. So, for example, you and a best friend could buy a duplex together, and you can each have your own space. Duplexes are not necessarily more expensive as a whole than a single-family home, and they are often less than condos, because you still have the responsibility of the exterior upkeep.

Townhomes

Another popular choice these days are townhomes, which are especially common in the suburbs. These are large developments (usually) with groups of homes that are attached to each other, so that each home shares one common wall with the home next to it. Townhomes can be smaller than the single-family homes around it, or they can be grander and more up-to-date than nearby homes that were built much earlier. Townhomes began as a cheaper alternative to single-family homes, but as buyers became more diverse and began to enjoy the benefits of a condominium structure (not having to mow the lawn, for example) townhome design became more sophisticated and expensive.

When you look at owning a townhome, you have to find out if the tax situation resembles the rowhouses built in the early part of the twentieth century, in which owners pay taxes on the house, as well as the land it sits on. These days, it is more common for townhomes to be part of a condominium structure, in which the owners pay taxes on the dwelling and then pay association fees for the upkeep of the land and exterior of the property.

If you are looking at both single-family homes and condos, townhomes, or co-ops, you need to talk to your lender about the types of loans they offer for each type of dwelling. Lenders don't always write the same kind of mortgages for these other types of homes the same way they do for single family homes.

First of all, lenders take into account how much any association fees would be, because the lender knows that the association fee will cut into the buyer's monthly budget. Second, they look at the health of the condo association to be sure money has been set aside for any unforeseen expenses.

Here's why: if a major repair is needed to fix a building or the property, the condo board may raise the association fees so much that it becomes difficult for an owner to pay both her mortgage and her fees. Unpaid association fees become liens against the property, which eventually becomes a problem for the mortgage lender.

Another problem could also arise that worries lenders. If major repairs are needed and the condo board can't afford to—or isn't responsible enough to—take care of them, then the value of the property goes down. So, you see, the lender isn't just taking a financial risk with you, but with the condo association or co-op board. For this reason, many lenders already have opinions about the condos, co-ops, and PUDS in their area. They already know, for instance, if the association or board is trustworthy.

In some parts of the country, mortgage lenders take steps to safeguard against these problems. They might ask borrowers to put a higher down payment on condo purchases. Likewise, some lenders feel more comfortable with co-ops, but buyers often don't. That's because, as co-owners in a corporation, if the co-op has a financial problem the owner is liable for that expense. These issues are very specific to different towns, cities, and areas. New York City lenders are used to co-op boards, since co-ops are a common type of ownership there. Townhomes are more common in suburbs and so lenders in those areas have usually researched the owners and directors of the townhome association.

Of course, none of these situations should be automatic deal breakers, and we aren't telling you about these situations to scare you away from any of them. Like the difference between colonial and contemporary homes, everyone has different needs and different financial tastes. The important thing is that you realize there are pros and cons to every home-buying situation, and you need to be sure that the type of property you're buying will suit you. If you're a woman who doesn't necessarily want to mow her own lawn or if you would like to own property and yet not live without nearby neighbors, then one of these options may suit you.

If you do look at condos, ask to see the minutes from the condo association's last two meetings. Read them carefully to get a sense of the financial health of the condo association, as well as of the general tone of the group. Is there anger or acrimony? Are the tenants worried about an upcoming large expense, such as a new roof or repaving of parking lots?

To figure out the cost of your principal, every $10,000 you borrow is equal to a payment of $27.77 per month over thirty years. So, a loan of $120,000 is $333.33 a month not counting interest, taxes, and other fees.

Getting Your Finances in Order

There are two categories of money you need to consider when you first start thinking about buying a home. You will need figure out how much you have for a down payment as well as how much you can afford in total monthly payments (not just in the mortgage, but the total PITI payment of principal, interest, taxes, and insurance).

So, to figure out your finances, you'll need to count up all the money you have. Chances are, you have a savings account, a checking account, maybe a 401(k) or other retirement fund, and maybe even some stocks and bonds in your name. You might also have a parent who has offered to lend you some money for your home. The first thing you need to do is make a list and know how much money is available to you for a down payment.

In a perfect world, you would have at least 20 percent of the total house cost for the down payment, but that isn't often the case anymore, especially now that homes are so expensive and women are buying them on their own at a younger age. So, don't worry if it seems like you don't have enough—once everything is written down and you've talked to some people you'll find that reality is more reassuring than speculation.

So, get out your notebook and write down what you have. And, if someone has promised you, or suggested to you, that she might help out in some way, don't be afraid to ask exactly what she meant. Is it a few hundred dollars or five thousand? That number is important to know, not only for you, but also to your lender, who will ask you this same question when you fill out your paperwork.

Prequalifying for a Loan

The first thing you need to know is that prequalifying and getting preapproval for a loan are two different things. Prequalifying is a first step, and it means that a lender has "roughly" said you can borrow a specific amount of money. Real estate agents and buyers will know the difference and will want to know if you have been preapproved, which carries much more weight.

Lenders prequalify you by looking at your income and your credit report and score, so they can tell roughly how much home you can afford. The lender is not offering you a loan or making a commitment to you.

When the lender is ready to preapprove, they will delve more deeply into your finances, finding out, for example, about any of your savings accounts or where you are getting your down payment money. When a lender has preapproved you, they are ready to write a letter to a seller, which will be submitted with the offer letter, saying that they are willing to give you a loan for the amount of money you are offering.

You can get preapproved even before you start looking at homes. This is a good idea, because, sometimes, you will prequalify for an amount that won't pan out in the preapproval process. You don't want to look for homes that, in actuality, you can't afford.

But here's another good reason for preapproval. When you prequalify, you aren't always being told what type of loan you can get. Perhaps you prequalify for a higher-interest loan than you would want to take out. During the preapproval process the lender will explain exactly what type of loan they are offering, which means you will know more specifically how much your payments will be and where that money will be going.

Neither a "preapproval" nor a "prequalification" are considered absolute loan commitments. What you need for a mortgage is a **final approval**, which requires a satisfactory inspection and title review, as well as no change in your financial status.

Your Credit Report and Credit Score

Two of the most important pieces of information a mortgage lender uses to determine if you are someone they want to lend money to and how much money they feel safe lending you are your credit report and your credit score.

The report that a creditor looks at has a detailed account of your spending history. In fact, in order to even have a credit report or score, you need to have at least one credit account six months or older. The lender will also consider something else: your credit score, which is sometimes called FICO for Fair, Isaac, Co., the company that developed the scoring. To make their jobs easier, creditors use a ranking system that gives them an idea of what your payment history is without them having to look at the details of your report.

If you read the previous sentence carefully, then we hope you see the problem—creditors look at your credit score and only when pressed will they look at your credit report carefully, which means that, unless your number is the one they are looking for, then it will be difficult for you to explain your credit history. Credit reporters and creditors simply use a programmed calculator to determine credit scores, which means a decision about your ability to purchase a home is being made by a computer, not a person. So, if you have questionable credit, you need to understand exactly what creditors are looking at and how to deal with a problematic system.

First, at this point in the booming credit history business, there are now two pre-eminent companies that create credit scores: FICO and Beacon (another company like Fair, Isaac). They have computer programs that take all of your payment histories and assign points to each piece of information. For example, if you make a payment on time, then you get a positive mark. If you are late, you get a negative number on the scorecard. Other positives include: not maxing out your cards, having long-standing and up-to-date accounts, and not having too many cards. Some negatives: charging the maximum amount available on a credit card, owing lots of money, and having too much available credit. Of course, how many credit cards is too many and how many is too few is a delicate balance and it's often tough for a consumer to figure out what they've done right and wrong.

Some other issues that are put into the computer: Any legal issues regarding money, such as a collection agency being called or a bankruptcy, your length of employment and residential history (the longer you've worked and lived in one place the better it looks to a lender).

The thing is, everything in this report is relative. If you have a long credit history with one negative item then chances are it won't look bad in the context of your report. If you have a short credit history with one late payment then it looks bad in the context of your report.

Check on your own credit

It's smart to run your credit report every six months or so—and therefore, at least six months before you even consider buying a house—so that you can clear up any problems before the bank looks at your report.

Once every item has a score, the system does a calculation and voila, you have a credit score.

According to lenders, these scores are a reliable indicator of whether or not someone will pay their mortgage on time. Of course, most people resent being assigned a number by a computer, and rightly so; most of these systems get a lot wrong on many of the reports they generate. Despite this, credit report agencies insist on their right to not reveal how these scores are computed even though they have an enormous impact on whether or not a consumer will get a loan and what interest rate they're offered.

The Credit Bureaus

There are three major credit reporting agencies who collect and sell the credit histories of all Americans. The agencies compete with each other and they have to make money from their reports, which means that, unfortunately for you, each company probably has a different version of your information. Therefore, you have to get your report from each company because you'll have to make sure that each report is correct.

The largest credit reporting agencies are Equifax, TransUnion, and Experian. However, there are also other, smaller credit reporting agencies, such as the check acceptance and verification credit bureaus Chexsystems, Certegy, and Tele-track. Likewise, there are tenant-screening agencies and a medical background organization called Medical Information Bureau or MIB. Lenders can call one, some, or all of these businesses to find out more about you.

Most of these businesses—and many other business—offer three-in-one credit reports or comprehensive credit reports for sale, but you don't need to pay for these. As of September 2005, every consumer has the right, by law, to get a credit report annually from each credit bureau without cost.

Here are phone numbers and Web sites for all of these businesses:

Equifax — www.equifax.com or call 800-685-1111
TransUnion — www.transunion.com or call 800-916-8800
Experian — www.experian.com or call 888-397-3742
Chexsystems — www.chexhelp.com or call 800-428-9623
Certegy — www.certegy.com or call 800-437-5120
Tele-track — www.teletrack.com or call 800-729-6981
MIB — www.mib.com or call 866-692-6901

A credit reporting agency will supply the online credit report with your credit history and personal information. Credit reporting agencies operate on a profit basis and charge to send out information to whoever wants it, which could be you, a lender, or anyone else.

Incorrect information on credit reports can cause problems for people. One of the most important laws that protects your identity and credit information is the Fair Credit Reporting Act. Its purpose is to promote the accuracy, fairness, and privacy of the information collected and maintained by credit reporting agencies.

If you are denied credit, employment, or insurance because of information in your report, the denying party must alert you and provide you with the name, address, and phone number of the credit reporting agency used to support the denial according to this law.

When you ask to see your credit report, the agency must give you all of the information in your file and a list of everyone who has requested it within the past sixty days. If you have been denied credit, employment, or insurance because of items in your file, you won't be charged to see your report as long as you make your request within sixty days of the problem.

If you find inaccuracies in your report, you have to do everything you can to fix the problem and the credit reporting agency must investigate those items. Then, the agency should send you a full copy of the investigation report. If you don't like the final conclusion, you can add a statement to your report to help you when you apply for a loan.

Whenever you apply for a loan, a mortgage, or a major purchase this information is submitted to the reporting agencies. If you used a different address then the reporting agencies would record that as if you have moved. Any inaccurate or misinformation must be reported to the credit reporting agencies so that your credit report can then be adjusted to reflect these changes.

Are you risky?

If you already own a home or have owned a home, you are generally considered a better loan risk.

More Details about Credit Scores

As we said, once the credit reporting company compiles all of your information, the numbers are run through a complex formula to determine your FICO (or Beacon) score. This three-digit, single number indicates your creditworthiness. A high FICO score means you're a better credit risk. The lower the score, the less you will be able to borrow. Also, interest rates and down payment amounts will most likely be higher with a lower credit score.

These are the potential numbers and scores:

- Less than 620—High risk
- 620 to 660—Uncertain
- 660 to 770—Reliable
- 720 or more—Very good
- Over 750—Excellent

Of course, different lending institutions give different weight to FICO scores. And they normally get the three scores from the three credit bureaus and take the middle number. And each credit bureau will give you a different number.

Working with credit is a balancing act. Excessive debt will lower your FICO score. Too little properly managed historical debt, paradoxically, also leads to lower FICO scores, as the credit reporting agency has nothing on which to base a report. According to some analysts, to produce the best FICO score, your total debt should be approximately half your revolving credit limit.

So, some debt isn't a bad thing, but for many of us, it's all too easy to get in over our heads financially. Following are some tips for repairing a bad credit rating, and maintaining a good one. If this sounds confusing, it is. However, as confusing as it is, it's important for you to always know your credit score and to rectify any problems or inaccuracies you notice.

Fixing Your Credit Report

The Fair Credit Reporting Act (FCRA) is a law that protects consumers from the improper use of credit information. If you are denied credit due to information contained in your credit report, you have the right to receive a free copy of the report. Take advantage of this, and check for inaccurate information or errors. Follow the dispute process indicated by the credit bureau. As long as your claim is reasonable, the credit reporting bureau must investigate your allegations within thirty days. Further, they must remove any negative entries if they cannot verify the information.

You may also dispute any claims directly with the source of information. If the information remains, you have the right to place an entry in your credit file with your side of the story. This, however, does not affect your credit score.

Information contained in the report is subject to time limitations. Any negative entries older than seven years must not be counted against you for financial purposes. Bankruptcies are an exception, and they remain if declared anytime within the last ten years.

Other consumer rights under the act include:

- Your consent is required for any reports for employers.
- Access to information is limited to valid financial agencies.
- Violators of the act may be sued for damages.

Don't get taken in by companies that offer to fix your bad credit. Like any other scenario, there are no quick fixes for credit problems. Jumping to new accounts and suddenly closing old ones will worsen your rating.

So, maintaining a good credit rating requires you to take an active role in your finances. Make sure you get annual reports from the three credit reporting agencies; that way you can check for inconsistencies and report mistakes promptly. Avoid the urge to spend more than you can afford to pay, and avoid applying for those unsolicited credit cards!

Your FICO score is affected most strongly by how well you handle the following:

- Status of your current accounts. Keep current with all your obligations for a strong FICO score. While mortgage payments count more than revolving debt or installment loans, your credit cards and car loans are the beginning of a beautiful FICO score.
- Your historical credit record. A strong, consistent record of paying your bills on time, and making all payments of installment plans, positively affects your credit score.

- Keeping a low balance on credit cards.
- Living at the same address for two or more years.

Negative factors include:

- Making multiple applications for credit over a short period of time.
- Moving a lot.
- Keeping high balances on credit cards.
- Having too many open accounts.

Is there another way I can figure out how much I can afford to pay for a house?

Monthly Rent x 200 = Home Price
This amount includes tax savings, so your monthly payment will still likely be higher than if you continued renting, but buying a house at this price won't put you further in debt or cause you problems.

Gifts

It's very common for first-time homebuyers to use gift money, i.e., money that is given to them without financial strings attached, to help pay for their house, specifically the down payment. If someone gives you a large sum of money for this purpose, you need to tell your mortgage lender.

The mortgage lender wants to know about gifts for a few reasons. First because they will be scrutinizing your finances very carefully, and they want to know that the down payment money isn't a loan that you're going to have to repay. Second because this will help them give you a loan of the correct amount. For example, if a house is $200,000 and your mother is going to give you $10,000 toward the down payment, then you will only need a mortgage for $190,000.

You will actually need to bring a letter saying that the money is a gift to your lender and to the close. The letter has to specify the amount of the gift and state that it doesn't have to be repaid.

I have atrocious credit and no job. Will anyone give me money? Why would they anyway?

MC Hammer, Willie Nelson, Donald Trump—all of these men, millionaires all—have declared bankruptcy at one time or another. It is not true that rich people have fewer financial problems than middle-class people. Some rich people overspend; rich people aren't always smart about money even. Some were born into it, some got lucky, and some will end up losing it.

On the flip side, there are postal workers who retire with millions in the bank because of intelligent saving and investing.

Therefore, the important thing isn't how much money you have, but how you handle it. So, if you have a lot of debt and no job, why would you want to buy a house? If your motives are to somehow improve your financial situation, then you need to be very clear about how you're going to make that happen.

Mortgage lenders want good customers. Even if you don't have a lot, the important thing is that you're a good borrower. And if you haven't been a good borrower, you can learn to be. Before you borrow more money why not learn how to save and improve your credit? Then, when you do go to buy a house, you will most likely get a better loan with a lower interest rate. And, more than that, you will have learned how to take good financial care of yourself, so that your home purchase doesn't become your next financial problem.

Affordability

We want to start this section with a caveat: It is not up to a mortgage broker, bank lender, or anyone else, to decide how much home you can afford.

Do not use a mortgage company or anyone who claims to be the final word on what you can borrow. Instead, remember they are telling you what you qualify to borrow. Any person or company with money to loan wants to lend you as much as you can possibly borrow, because then you will pay more in interest and other fees over a longer period of time, although they will also only lend you what they believe you can be relied on to pay back.

Mortgage lenders tell you how much you qualify for and can afford based on your credit and your repayment history. They won't lend you what they think you can't handle. On the other hand, the bottom line is that it is up to you to determine how much you feel you can comfortably pay each month. You—not the bank or the mortgage company—are in control of how you spend your money, so even though the financial organization wants to offer you money, don't assume that it's in your best interest to take all they are offering.

On the other hand, the only way you'll be able to get the house you want is with the right loan, so you do have to work well with the financial people in order to borrow the right amount of money and work out a repayment schedule that won't cause you stress and will get you the house you want to live in.

As we wrote this book, the average home in San Francisco, California, cost over a million dollars while the average home in Birmingham, Alabama, was approximately $150,000. Then, there are all those houses and condos in between, and that includes, of course, inexpensive homes in San Francisco and million-dollar mansions in Birmingham.

We bring this up because price is somewhat relative based on the very specific place you want to live. However, some things—how much money you have available and how much a home costs, for example—are realities. The equations and financial understanding that you need for any given house do not change even if the specific dollar amounts do.

While it's fun to look at (and dream about) five-million-dollar mansions in ritzy communities, we designed this book to help you actually buy a house that you can afford and feel good about. Buying a home that you can't afford is not a good idea. For one thing, stressing about a mortgage payment (or worse, defaulting on a mortgage loan) is an awful experience. Second, one of the most significant benefits of home buying is that, eventually (if you want to and if you do handle your finances properly), you can trade up and possibly buy that dream home. So, keep tearing out those pictures from *Architectural Digest*—one day that skylit contemporary on the Pacific Coast might really be yours.

To figure out what you can afford, you need to know:

- How much cash you have for the down payment, as well as for the costs involved, such as closing and other fees.
- What your monthly take-home pay is, as well as how much other income you have available to you on a steady and reliable basis.
- How much of that available money you want to, and can, spend on a mortgage. For example, if you have outstanding loans or debt or if you want a certain amount available for other expenses, then you need to factor that amount into your budget.
- Your credit score. Your credit score will determine how much the bank or mortgage lender will charge in interest. And the interest rate will greatly affect the amount of the monthly check you write.

There are two equations that will give you a very rough idea of what you might be comfortable spending when you buy a house. First, in an ideal situation, your expected housing costs—namely, the mortgage principal, interest, taxes, and homeowner's insurance (PITI)—shouldn't exceed 28 percent of your income, although many lenders may allow up to 33 percent.

The housing expenses equation

You can use this equation to help determine how much you can spend each month for your entire mortgage payment (PITI), including the principal, interest, taxes, and insurance:

Yearly Income: $72,000   Gross Monthly Income: $6,000
  28% = $1,680   33% =$1,980

Going by the 28 percent rule, you could pay $1,680 for PITI, including $150 in taxes and $50 in insurance. So you would have $1,480 available for a mortgage payment at 7 percent for a 30-year fixed rate. That means you could afford a $222,450 house, and you would still have $4,320 to pay your monthly debt bill (credit cards, car, student loans, etc.).

The second equation is a debt-to-income ratio. Ideally, your total monthly debt—including your expected housing costs plus credit card bills and loan payments—shouldn't exceed 38 percent of your gross income, and preferably not more than 36 percent.

Now, there's lots of wiggle room in these equations, so don't panic if you fill in your numbers and find you can only afford a one-room shack. These days there are loans and programs to help almost everyone buy a house, so the equations above are most useful if you plan to take out a traditional 30-year mortgage with a 20 percent down payment.

We're about to explain what you'll be paying for when you take out a mortgage. Because, while you need to know all of the information we mentioned above to determine how much you can spend on a house, there's an important flip side to this information—you need to know what you're going to be paying for.

Down Payment, Recurring Costs, and Nonrecurring Costs

At some point since you've begun to think about buying a home, you've heard the terms down payment, closing costs, and mortgage. Those terms are not interchangeable. They each have a specific meaning and pay for a specific part of the house that you are buying.

The down payment is a lump sum that decreases the amount of the loan you will have to take out. For example, let's say you want to purchase a home that is $300,000. If you have $50,000 to put toward the purchase of that home, you will only have to take out a loan for $250,000, which means your mortgage payments will be less money each month. Down payments typically range from 3 percent to 20 percent of the house price. While there are programs that allow for 0 percent down payment, as well as ways to put more money down, this range is the most common.

The down payment is an important part of your financial deal, as well as important information for the lender (who will use that information to help determine your creditworthiness) and the seller (who might want a buyer who is able to put down a good-sized down payment). If you've got the money, there are advantages to putting 20 percent down, because then you immediately have substantial equity in your home—you're investing cash. This may be important to you psychologically, and that counts. In addition, you'll avoid having to pay private mortgage insurance.

Sellers want buyers who can make large down payments because little-cash-down financing can be risky. If a buyer has little or no money of her own invested in a property, the lender bases the risk of the loan both on the buyer's creditworthiness, as we said, and on the appraisal of the property when deciding whether or not to make the loan.

They do this because a buyer with less money down is more likely to skip out on the loan. Lenders usually have the right to take over the property if the buyers stop making their mortgage payments. This is the last thing a lender wants to do. A large down payment serves as a strong incentive for the borrowers to keep the mortgage payments current rather than risk losing their investment in a foreclosure.

Because of this risk in a low-down-payment situation, the appraisal becomes important because it provides confirmation that if the buyer defaults and the lender has to foreclose on the property and resell it, the property will sell for enough to cover the mortgage amount. When a lender offers a no- or low-cash-down deal, there's little margin for error in terms of the value of the property.

Of course, some buyers make low-cash-down offers because they have no choice. They have limited liquid assets. Other buyers are capable of making larger down payments, but they prefer not to for tax reasons. These are usually high-income individuals who are looking for the maximum tax write-off possible. (Mortgage interest on a primary residence is tax-deductible.) They also may have better use for their cash, such as other business investments.

You cannot tell a seller that you have money to put down when you are actually borrowing the down payment money. This is known as 100 percent financing, and the seller can back out if you aren't completely up-front about this.

In today's world, lots of buyers use 100 percent financing and borrow their down payment money, but this never used to be done (which is just one reason it was so difficult to buy a house).

Of course, the best reason to put down a large down payment is so your monthly mortgage payment won't be too high and so you can avoid paying mortgage insurance (which protects the lender).

If you are putting down a small amount of money, you might want to include your credit score (if it is high) in your preapproval letter. This shows that even if you weren't able to save a lot of money, you are responsible and reliable.

If you are in a multiple offer situation, low- or no-cash-down financing is often an unattractive quality in an offer. Ask your agent to provide comparable sales information (comps) so the lender and seller can see that the property would resell (if necessary) easily for the purchase price. Finally, if you have the ability and inclination to do so, offer to make a larger cash down payment if the appraisal comes in for less than the purchase price. Put this information in your offer letter and use it during the negotiation process.

In addition, some mortgage providers give a lower interest rate if you make more than the minimum required down payment.

Closing Costs

It's ironic that just as you're beginning the process of buying a home, everyone you talk to is going to mention "closing costs." This is an important term that you need to know and understand. Closing costs comprise the final amount of money you're agreeing to pay when you buy your house. Some of these payments are made at the signing of the contract, while others will be made over time. For example, you'll pay the inspector right away, but you'll pay the mortgage over fifteen or thirty years. These are called "nonrecurring closing costs" and "recurring closing costs."

Your lender will usually prepare a "good faith estimate" of your closing costs so that you will have a very general idea of how much you're going to spend before you close the deal. However, you won't know the exact amount of all of your closing costs until you're at the table with a pen in your hand.

Sometimes lenders will give you this estimate as soon as possible after they have okayed your loan, but they are only required to mail it to you within three business days of application. They aren't required to list all the potential costs, and they also don't even know what all the costs will actually be (such as how much a notary public might charge), so don't rely on this number; just use it as a guideline.

Although the lender will prepare this estimate, she and her company aren't the only people who are going to get your money. There are two types of closing costs: Recurring (they happen every month) and nonrecurring (one time only). Some are factored in your loan, while others aren't.

Recurring Closing Costs That You Will Pay the Lender

- Private mortgage insurance (PMI)—If you put down less than 20 percent of the total cost of your house, the mortgage company may ask you to pay insurance on your mortgage. This is called PMI, and it protects the company in case you default on your loan.
- Mortgage principal and interest—You will pay your first month at signing, so you'll need your checkbook handy with the amount ready for the lender.
- Property taxes and homeowner's insurance—You pay your property taxes through your escrow account, an account where the bank holds money of yours for that purpose, as part of your monthly mortgage check. Nevertheless, you'll have to have the money for your first month's payment of property taxes upon signing the contract. You pay your homeowner's insurance on your own; you should pay it as soon as possible, too, because accidents can happen during the move.

Nonrecurring Costs That May Be Factored into Your Loan Approval But Aren't Paid to the Lender

- Maintenance and repairs—Depending on the deal you make with the seller, you may have to either pay for some repairs or be paid for repairs. Also, if you are buying a condo, co-op, or townhome, you'll need to figure in the cost of the monthly maintenance. If you think you might need help with some of the chores of homeownership (such as lawn maintenance, snowplowing, or caring for the house, such as gutters and regular repairs) then you need to make sure you have money set aside for this. Make sure you include it in your budget.
- Appliances and furniture—Unlike renting an apartment, buying a home means you're also paying for the large appliances inside it, such as refrigerators, washer, dryer, dishwasher, and, if you're going to do your own home care, tools, lawn mowers, etc. These are pricey items, and you need to make sure you take them into consideration.
- Renovations—Many of us love not only the house we are buying, but our vision of the house we think we can turn it into: We imagine new paint and cabinets in the kitchen

or better tiles in the bathroom. Once again, these items are not cheap, and you need to figure their cost into your budget.

Nonrecurring Closing Costs

These expenses are fees that the lender charges for loaning you the money. (We know, you'd think the interest would be enough for them!) Of course, each lender is different, but this is a list of fees that you might see on your final bill. By the way, lenders have to list every single amount they are charging you for, and you can negotiate away—or at least you can try to—some of these fees, so be sure to speak up if you see something that doesn't make sense or if you think an amount isn't fair.

- **Loan origination fee or "points"**—You can negotiate points and interest rates with your lender. One point is equal to one percent of the mortgage loan, and if you can pay more in points, then you get a lower interest rate. If you have a VA or FHA loan, you pay one point as the loan origination fee. So, the loan origination fee is normally listed as one point or one percent of the loan within the amount the lender cites. Any points added to the loan origination fee are called "discount points." On a conventional loan, discount points are usually lumped in with the loan origination fee. These points aren't really discounts, because you're still paying an amount of money up-front, but they are taking away interest that would be a part of your loan.

Why should I consider paying points?

Buyers often choose to pay a one-time charge called mortgage "points" in exchange for a lower interest rate. Usually paid at closing, each point costs 1 percent of the mortgage amount, or $2,000 on a $200,000 loan. The lower rate reduces the monthly mortgage payment, and points paid in conjunction with the purchase of a home are generally tax-deductible in the year they're paid (see a tax advisor). Monthly savings will often exceed what you paid in points in just a few years' time. However, many real estate agents will advise you to not pay points and to instead shop for a better rate, using an offer you've seen with points as your bargaining chip. Points give the lenders more money up-front, but you can simply use that cash as part of your down payment, which lowers the amount you are borrowing in the first place.

- **Appraisal fee**—Your home and the property it sits on are also the collateral you are using for your loan. In other words, the bank or mortgage lender will use the value of your home and property as insurance if you default on your loan (so that, if you do, they can resell it to pay themselves back). Therefore, they will make sure that the house and the land is worth what you're borrowing for it. Appraisal fees vary, based on location and size of home.

- **Credit report**—You should have gotten a copy of your credit report for yourself before you started applying for loans. Your lender will also want this, so offer them a copy of what you have. Otherwise they will run the report themselves, which can cost $20 for each credit bureau.

- **Inspection fee**—If you are building a new home, the lender might want to inspect the property as it is being built and when the property is finished. If so, you may be charged for both. This is sometimes called a 442 inspection. Inspection fees are added for existing homes, and the buyer is usually required to pay for it, but generally the lender doesn't charge a great deal for it.

- **Mortgage broker fee**—Mortgage brokers handle most mortgages, and these brokers charge a fee for their services. The amount you are paying for this service should be listed on your contract. Wholesale lenders (such as those online) offer lower rates and "no-cost" loans because you aren't paying a broker.

- **Tax service fee**—Your mortgage lender may charge you to keep track of whether you're paying your property taxes (because if you're not, you will be liable for those expenses before you are liable for your mortgage payments). This is usually less than $100.

- **Flood certification/monitoring**—Your lender will pay to find out if you live in a flood zone (which is designated by the government), and they charge you for this service. The lender updates this information and will continue to charge you for it periodically over the years.

- **Document preparation**—Lenders will sometimes pass on the cost of their processing to you, the lendee. It usually costs a few hundred dollars and will be listed on your loan.

- **Underwriting fee**—Although the underwriter (the person who actually writes the loan and makes the credit decision about the buyer) is usually the mortgage broker, sometimes the company hires a contract underwriter, and they will charge you for this. This can cost a few hundred dollars. Find out if the lender has one on staff and ask if there is a fee for this. However, the lender may then charge a "processing fee" which is an underwriting fee in disguise. Once again, ask about this ahead of time.

There are many other charges that the lender might label with high-falutin'-sounding names in order to make them seem nonnegotiable, but don't be intimidated by this. Question everything you don't understand, and remember, everything is a negotiation. These are some of the terms you might see (or you might see terms with words similar to these in them):

- **Appraisal review fee**—Some lenders tell you they will conduct appraisals over the years, especially on more expensive properties, although they charge you for this before the appraisals occur. The fee for each appraisal can be from one hundred to several hundred dollars, depending on the property.
- **Wire transfer fee**—Rather than actually handing you a check, lenders now transfer the money electronically (over what used to be called "the wire") and they charge you for doing this.
- **Moving expenses**—Most likely, the lender will not include this amount in its estimate, however, if you are moving a long distance, moving a lot of furniture, or simply have to hire someone to move you, don't neglect to figure this into your closing costs. A move can cost anything from a few hundred dollars (even if you're just paying the gas, beer, and pizza expenses for your friends) to many thousands of dollars, and you need to figure that expense into your budget.

Money You Pay in Advance

You're going to end up writing a check at your closing for a variety of expenses. This is what people mean when they remind you of the need for money for "closing costs." This money will cover one-time expenses that aren't included in your monthly mortgage payment.

- **Prepaid interest**—Mortgage loans are usually due on the first of each month, but if you sign your mortgage loan on the fifteenth of the month, you have to pay the rest of the month's interest to get the interest paid up to the first at the closing.
- **Homeowner's insurance**—This is a legal necessity, and you won't be able to sign your loan agreement without proof of insurance because the truth is, the mortgage lender owns your home for the first few years at least (because you're mostly paying interest, not principal), and they want to make sure their investment is protected. Homeowner's insurance covers any possible damages that happen to your home and the items in it. When you buy a house, you typically pay the first year's insurance when you close the transaction, and that can be a substantial amount of money. If you're

buying a condominium, your association fees usually cover this insurance. (Remember, though, that you still need a policy then for your interior, since the association insurance only covers the exterior.)

- **VA funding fee**—If you're taking out a Veterans Administration loan, the VA charges a fee for guaranteeing your loan. If you have not used your VA eligibility in the past, the fee is 2 percent of the loan balance. If you have used your VA eligibility before, it is 3 percent of the loan. If you are refinancing from a VA loan to a VA loan, it is .75 percent of the loan amount. Veterans have an alternative to paying this fee as a one-time expense, however. They can finance it and add it to their loan balance, which is why the loan balance on VA loans can be higher than the actual purchase amount.

- **Up-front mortgage insurance premium (UFMIP)**—This charge is currently 2.25 percent of the loan balance and is only required on single-family residences (SFRs) or Planned Unit Developments (PUDs), not on condo purchases. Like the VA funding fee, it is normally added to the balance of the loan (so you pay it each month rather than at closing). However, unlike a VA loan, the buyer must then add another fee on top of this: a monthly mortgage insurance fee. This is why FHA loans sound great at first, but many lenders don't recommend them, especially if a homebuyer can get a conventional loan.

- **Private mortgage insurance (PMI)**—If a lender considers you a high-risk or if you put a very low down payment on the house, then lenders will ask you to pay insurance on their loan. Mortgage insurance protects the lender if you default on your loans. Most mortgage insurance is paid along with the monthly mortgage payment, but some first-time homebuyer programs still require the first year mortgage insurance premium to be paid in advance.

Fees add up

Remember, a few ongoing fees of $50 or $60 will significantly change what your total monthly payment is. We know one woman who figured out her mortgage as $1,000 a month and was stunned when it turned out to be $1,150 each month. That can really change your budget. So, before you sign anything, ask your lender to call you when she has a final figure so you can be sure you know what you're looking at.

Reserves Deposited with Lender

If you make a very small down payment, your lender may require you to deposit funds into an escrow or impound account. This money is yours, but the lender can use it to make your insurance, property tax, and mortgage insurance payments or any combination of these three things. Then, each month, you deposit additional funds into your impound account, as well as paying your mortgage. This is one way the lender stays one step ahead of you (and guarantees that you won't skip out on a month's payment).

Some lenders will actually give you a reduced loan origination fee if you choose to set up an impound account. But don't sign up for this agreement without thinking it through, as there are other ways to invest this money (which might total a few hundred dollars or more).

To determine how much money needs to be put into escrow or the impound account for insurance, your lender will divide your annual premium by twelve. This will be the monthly amount you'll deposit. A lender can keep two months of reserves in your account, so you'll have to deposit two months' payment to start the program.

If your lender requires the property tax to be put into an escrow account, your payment will be determined by when you close your real estate transaction. You have to pay property tax for the part of the year in which you live in the home, based on when the taxes are due. So, make sure you ask about when property taxes are due in the town you're moving into.

If you need to pay mortgage insurance, your lender may ask you to keep those funds in an escrow account. The lender can have you put two months' worth of mortgage insurance as an initial deposit into the impound account.

What You Will Pay For

- **Title insurance**—This guarantees that the new homeowner has clear title to the property.
- **Your lawyer**—You have to pay the real estate lawyers. Be sure you find out ahead of time what they charge and include those amounts when determining your closing cost budget.

- **Pest inspection**—Also referred to as a termite inspection. This inspection tests not only for pest infestations, but also other items such as wood rot and water damage. The inspection usually runs around $75. If repairs are required, the amount to cover those repairs can vary. The seller will usually pay for the most serious repairs, but this is a negotiable item. Usually (not always) the pest inspection fee is paid by the seller of the home and is not normally reflected on the good faith estimate.
- **Home inspection**—You will pay this money directly to the inspector.
- **Home warranty**—This policy covers major appliances and other items included in your home purchase if they break down within the time period specified in the contract.

Bank and Lender Fees

Your lender doesn't just charge you for the loan itself. The company will also include fees in its bill to cover the expense of processing your loan. You will usually see a phrase such as "closing/escrow/settlement fee" that will comprise these expenses. In the end you will be paying for:

- **Notary fees**—Most loan documents must be notarized, and the notary will charge you for this service. It's usually less than $50.
- **Recording fees**—The county or local government will charge you to record and file the new records. The fees vary, but are usually less than $100.
- **Sub-escrow fee**—The title insurance company may charge you for the title search and other work it does to prepare for the closing.
- **Messenger or courier fees**—You might be responsible for paying all of the charges associated with sending contracts by messenger, mail, or FedEx all between the lender, title company, escrow account, and other professionals. This can add up. Find out ahead of time if you're paying these fees.

Condo transaction fees

If you're buy a condo or a home within a planned or gated community, you may have to pay an association fee or a homeowners' transaction fee. Be sure to find out about these fees when talking to the association.

Don't forget the furniture

It is very easy to get into serious debt when you buy a house because of the joy of redecorating and furnishing your very own home. While you should certainly buy what you need to be comfortable and happy, try not to make your life miserable by running up your credit cards. Remember, you're going to be in this house for a long time, so you have plenty of time to get the things you want without making your life miserable trying to pay bills that you didn't count on having.

Location, Location, Location

You might not think that the "location" concern pertains to you. Perhaps you know you want to live near your family or in the city where you have a job. But, as you may have heard, the three most important words in real estate are "location, location, location." What does that mean? It means that the value of your home is directly related to where it's located. Sometimes location refers to a town, sometimes location refers to a region, and sometimes location refers to one street.

But what "location" specifically refers to are the things you can't change about a house, i.e., the problems—or benefits—of where it's located. Because you can't change the location of a house (unless it's an extreme situation), location becomes much of what you're really paying for. Three bedrooms with a view of the ocean often is worth more than three bedrooms with no view. Three bedrooms located close to the office may be worth more to you—and others—than three bedrooms two hours from the city.

Of course, at the same time, those same three bedrooms away from the city must also have good surroundings. Most people don't want to live near railroad tracks, factories, or next door to a fire or police station. On the other hand, if you live far from basic amenities such as a grocery store, a mall, and a quality healthcare facility, that can also have a negative impact on the property's value.

This is a list of what real estate agents and buyers generally consider to be poor locations:

- Near train tracks or a train yard
- Right next to convenience stores or strip malls
- Near garbage dumps or recycling stations
- Close to nightclubs or restaurants that stay open late
- Near highways or entrances to highways
- Right next to a school
- In a town or city that is having significant financial problems
- In bad school districts
- Being a single-family home near an apartment complex
- Any high-crime neighborhood

There's one more thing we want to say about location: You need to tell your real estate agent what locations work for you. If you don't want to be on a main street or in a neighborhood with a lot of kids, or perhaps you don't like houses without trees in the yard. Just as you like certain aspects of houses and dislike others, you will also feel the same thing about locations.

A good real estate agent, by the way, will be happy to drive you around town to see different neighborhoods and hear more about the different sections, both their benefits and drawbacks. Remember, too, that just because you go into the home-buying process with an idea of what you want, that doesn't mean your opinion and desire won't change over time. As you learn more about the pluses (and minuses) of homes, don't be surprised if your lists of wants and needs adapt to what you're told about different houses. Connect with a real estate agent who you've heard has worked with types of homes you're interested in. Ask friends if they can recommend a real estate agent they've dealt with.

I'm not sure how long I want to live in this new house. Is that okay?

This is a very legitimate concern, because with all of the money you will be putting into your home, such as inspection, taxes, closing costs, you don't get it all back in equity or tax refunds right away. Buying a home that you plan to own (unless you're going to fix it and resell it or try to flip it, see Chapter 7) only for six months might not be a wise choice. Buying a home costs money even if you're putting no money down.

But if you plan to stay in your home—or at least the area—for a few years then you might find the investment worth it. We put a calculator in the back of this book for you to plug in the numbers of renting versus buying (see "Should I Rent? Live at Home? Or Buy?" in Part 3). Be sure to include all of the potential closing costs.

Chapter 2

The People You'll Meet

You saw a house you like, and you called the phone number listed on the sign stuck into the owner's front lawn. You get the main number of a real estate office and end up talking to someone whose name isn't on the sign, but who offers to show you the house anyway. Is this who you're supposed to be talking to? Are you supposed to hire a real estate agent to help you find a house or should you just keep calling these phone numbers on the signs?

But, wait, you're not done with the questions. When you finally meet with the real estate agent of a house you're interested in, she immediately tells you that not only does she know someone who handles mortgages, but she also knows an inspector. Who are these people and what are you supposed to do with them?

Buying a home is a personal decision, but it involves lots of people, many of whom you haven't met yet. This can be intimidating, because each of these people has a specialty—mortgages, construction, the law—and you are someone who most likely has very little knowledge in these areas. The important thing to remember is that these experts are exactly that: experts. It is their business to help you get the house or loan or insurance you need to live happily.

Therefore, your job is twofold. First, you have to use your instinct about which of these people you can trust and seem the most knowledgeable. Do not ignore your instincts about anyone or their motives. Remember, the seller's real estate agent is working for the seller, the mortgage lender is working for the mortgage company, and the lawyers are working for the law firms. In other words, the only person who is looking out for you alone is you. Even a real estate agent you hire to represent you is still being paid on commission, therefore, it is in her best interest to find a house for you no matter what.

Now, of course, we gave you this warning (very Daddy-like of us, we think) but, for the most part, we believe, like Anne Frank said, that people are good. Even lawyers. So, we aren't telling you not to trust this group of professionals you'll hire to help you. We are only reminding you not to trust anyone blindly. Do your homework by reading this book and understanding what each of these people can and can't do, and then listen to your gut. If one of the people you meet with makes you uncomfortable, feel free to ask to speak to someone else or find another professional. Or at least get a second opinion. Ask around of friends and people you know who've already purchased a home in your area, and see who they might recommend to help answer your concerns. Remember, as Big Bird says, asking questions is the best way to get answers.

Real Estate Agents

In our view, sometimes it's hard to remember that a real estate agent has a job to do and a life of her own, because one general statement we feel safe making about real estate agents is that they are always on call. If you call a real estate agent on a Sunday, she'll talk to you. If you call her at night, she'll talk to you. She'll give you her cell phone number and her home number and generally make herself available to you. Does she do this because she's the nicest person in the world? Possibly. But it's more likely that your real estate agent does this because she has a hard job and the industry is that competitive.

We're going to tell you two things about real estate agents in this section. First, we're going to explain a little about what their job is like (just so you have an idea of what you're dealing with), and second, we're going to tell you what a real estate agent can and can't, as well as should and shouldn't, do for you.

The first thing you need to know is that anyone who advertises herself as a real estate agent or real estate broker in the United States has passed a rigorous exam and received a license to practice. But, of course, being a good real estate agent doesn't only involve understanding real estate laws and real estate practice. Most real estate agents have other important skills, such as being able to understand what people need and listen to their desires. Remember, many buyers can't really describe what they're looking for—it's so specific to each person and what one person calls cozy another person would call small and dark.

Real estate brokers and real estate agents are different. A broker has passed a separate test. An agent has to work for a broker for two years before she can apply for a broker's exam. Then the broker has to get bonded because she is responsible for the agents who work for her.

Nevertheless, brokers and agents both understand the market in which they sell houses. They need to be able to price houses in a way that will sell, but that will also make the seller some money. They need to understand zoning and tax laws. They need to know who offers good financing and who will help their clients get through the process easily, but legally. Real estate agents and brokers also need to be good negotiators, because they act as intermediaries between buyers and sellers.

Most agents work as on a contract basis with real estate brokers who are part of a real estate company, such as Century 21. When the real estate agent sells a house or helps a buyer purchase a home, they receive a portion of the commission on the sale. As a buyer, you do not necessarily have to pay a commission if your agent helps you find a house. It's the seller who signs an agreement to pay a commission to their agent, who may or may not split the commission with the buying agent.

Some of the things brokers and agents do to earn their commission is bring buyers and sellers together through advertisements and meetings, explain properties and sale details to the involved parties, arrange for title searches, and sometimes help with financing details and closings.

Much of a real estate agent's time is spent doing leg work—finding properties to sell or buy, for example. When they find a property to sell, real estate agents do some research about similar homes to see what the best asking price would be. If a real estate agent is working on behalf of a buyer, then they look for homes that match what the buyer says she is looking for. In both cases, the real estate agents get commissions for a final sale or purchase.

Some real estate agents help to buy and sell commercial real estate, such as office buildings, large plots of land, or farms. Whatever their particular specialty, real estate agents need to understand the market and the laws about those types of properties.

In some states, homebuyers must sign a statement saying they are only working with one real estate agent, and the real estate agent must also state that they will work on the behalf of both the buyer and seller so that they both get a fair deal.

Once a deal is in place, a real estate agent has to make sure both parties meet all the terms of the contract before the closing date. This can mean following up on inspections, meetings with lenders, and other items agreed upon by those involved, such as any repairs to the home.

When you deal with real estate agents, you may be dealing with a national or regional real estate company, such as RE/MAX. Some of these companies are franchises or parent companies. However, each agent and broker has passed a test and is licensed by the state and responsible for living up to the state's regulations.

Real estate agents must be high school graduates, at least eighteen years old, and pass an extensive examination. Plus, they must be licensed by their state and thus usually take classes for at least a couple of days a year to stay up-to-date. Some agents and brokers earn a bachelor's degree in real estate.

The real estate agent you use should do a number of things. First, she should understand exactly what you're looking for and have a good sense of who you are and your priorities. She should understand whether a fireplace is more important to you than an office or whether you're willing to pay more for mature landscaping. She should have a sense of what is completely unacceptable to you—such as a home that needs extensive renovations or a house in a bad neighborhood.

Agents and brokers are particularly important if you are moving to an area with which you aren't that familiar; for example, if you're moving to a new state or even a town where you don't know the schools or the neighborhoods. And, by the way, even if you don't have kids, the school district a home is in is very important to its resale value, so you'll want to pay attention to a school's ranking, as this will help determine how much your house is worth.

By looking at her multiple listing service (MLS) an agent will be able to tell you:

1. A list of all the homes available, specifically those in your price range, with photos of the exterior, as well as, sometimes, pictures of the interior.
2. Each home's description, such as number of rooms, year it was built, square footage, and the amount of the most recent tax bill.
3. How long the home has been on the market and its original asking price (if the price has been reduced).
4. The name of the listing broker and the directions to the house.
5. Comps, i.e., a list of comparable homes and their selling price.

You can look at the MLS, too, on a number of Web sites, but the Web sites are not updated as quickly as a local real estate agent can find out about a particular house. It's best for you to use a combination of your own research and your real estate agent's expertise and knowledge.

You might also consider trying to find a real estate agent who specializes in helping women buying their first homes or women dealing with the aftermath of a divorce (or whatever your situation is). Agents can actually earn certification in specific populations, such as retirement buying or first-time home buying. One of the best ways to find this type of real estate agent is to ask a friend who is in a situation similar to yours.

We also want to warn you to beware of pushy real estate agents. In some states, real estate agents are required to ask you to sign a contract saying that they are representing you for a certain amount of time. The contract can cover any period of time, such as one day, one house visit, or up to a few months or a year. Although this contract is required by law because it is designed to protect you, the buyer, from having a real estate agent represent the seller and you at the same time, you also want to make sure you don't sign up with a real estate agent you don't like or trust. If a real estate agent pressures you to sign a contract that you don't want to sign, don't sign it and tell her you are more than happy to call another real estate agent. Any real estate agent can show you a house that is on the market. However, if you find a real estate agent you like and trust, feel free to sign the contract for the time period you are comfortable with.

Mortgage Lenders

There are two general types of mortgage lenders: mortgage brokers and mortgage bankers. Mortgage broker firms are generally smaller than banks. Brokers don't actually lend the money, but find the best deals from lenders for buyers based on their specific needs and situations. Mortgage brokers understand the business of mortgages and can help you look at all of your options and offer you their knowledge about the different loans available.

Mortgage banks, on the other hand, are usually large and more corporate; sometimes your local branch is part of a larger institution. Mortgage banks can also broker loans for other banks or investors, although, in some cases, loan officers are limited in the number and types of mortgage products she can offer.

Sometimes a mortgage broker is called a loan officer or loan originator. Whatever their title, mortgage brokers aren't required to get any training or be licensed, so you need to make sure you find a reputable one.

The first thing a loan officer usually does is prequalify a borrower. Then, once they have an idea of how much money the borrower will need and can comfortably obtain, they complete the loan application process with them. The loan officer's main job, however, is to handle the problem solving and answer any questions the lender and borrower have.

Real estate agents and builders generally know and have relationships with loan officers, but you should shop around for the right mortgage broker, no matter who recommends someone, because it's important that you feel your lender is on your side, not on the side of the others involved in the negotiation.

Often mortgage brokers specialize in specific types of loans, so if you are in a certain circumstance (such as needing an FHA loan) make sure the person you work with has experience in that area.

If you have a relationship with a bank or credit union, first consider speaking to a loan officer in that organization (if they offer mortgages). If you belong to any type of professional organization or union, find out if that entitles you to talk with a mortgage broker affiliated with that group.

Finally, if you have credit issues, consider finding a broker who specializes in nonconforming loans, which is sometimes called subprime lending.

Along with the mortgage broker, you might also meet a processor and underwriter. The processor's role is to complete the loan file for review by the underwriting department. A processor accumulates the detailed paperwork required for loan approval. Processors are generally very knowledgeable about loan programs and the required documentation; they usually possess excellent customer service skills. The underwriter issues the formal loan approval on behalf of the lender and bears the responsibility for understanding and communicating investor guidelines with respect to each transaction. The underwriter makes the final decision as to whether or not the loan is granted and under what conditions the transaction can close.

Finally, you may have to work with someone who closes the mortgage loan. This person is called a "closer" and is common only in certain parts of the country. The closer formally transfers the ownership of the property from one person or entity to another. The closer ensures that the title is free from encumbrances (that the property can, in fact, be legally transferred from one individual or entity to another) and understands the complex process necessary to effect the settlement.

Attorneys and real estate agents become experts in understanding the title to the property and in related legal matters. They frequently do the work needed to clear the title when there are different filings of record that would prevent the sale or transfer of real property.

Some states require escrow companies close loan transactions; a closer can work toward becoming an escrow officer or escrow department manager. Other states require attorneys to close loan transactions, or sometimes a closing assistant may also perform the function of or move into the role of a paralegal.

Sellers (Who Are Selling Their Own Homes)

For the most part, buyers and sellers don't meet until they're both at the closing table. So chances are you won't have to deal with the seller at all. However, these days more and more sellers are skipping the real estate agent and taking care of business themselves. So, if that's the case, the seller is not only the person saying goodbye to their home, but the person who wants to save the 6 percent commission fee most real estate agents charge.

"For Sale by Owner" homes, or FSBOs (sometimes pronounced "fizz-bo"), are becoming more common as sellers begin to feel more comfortable using the Internet to advertise their homes and the paperwork is more readily available to anyone who needs it. But owners don't only use the Internet to list their homes. You'll see signs out front with "For Sale by Owner" on the lawn, and many of these sellers list their homes in local newspapers.

So, how do you deal with a person who is selling his—or her—own house?

That may depend on why you suspect someone is selling her house herself. There are a number of reasons a person or couple may choose to sell a house on their own, but you can pretty much bet it's not because they find the process fun. In fact, it's a pretty good guarantee that the person is doing it to save money.

So, where does that leave you, the potential buyer?

Well, looking around the house will give you a sense of whether the seller needs the money quickly (or would maybe want a larger down payment) or whether he is selling the home on his own because he's in no rush to get out and figures he has enough time to not worry about the 6 percent he would have to give to the real estate agent. Or, perhaps he has unrealistic expectations and thinks his house is worth more than he can get for it.

In a hot housing market, you'll need to best figure out how to make an offer that the owner can't refuse, but that, at the same time you can live with (for thirty years). If you're working with an agent, she'll be able to talk you through what you can put into your offer. For example, if you notice the home needs works done on the exterior or if the cabinetry is old, you can use this in your offer letter to explain why your offer is lower than the asking price.

However, you want to be complimentary and kind, not insulting. Explain the issues in a nonjudgmental and detached way. And write everything down in your offer letter so that you are both clear about the terms.

When you write an offer letter and give it to an owner, you typically include earnest money, which proves you are serious about the deal. This is typically $1,000—not a small amount of money. This money should be deposited into an escrow account with a third party so that you don't lose your money should a disagreement arise. We can't emphasize enough the need for you to have a real estate lawyer before signing anything. This is especially true if no real estate agent is involved.

Real Estate Web Sites and Resources

Like most industries, real estate has changed dramatically because of the Web. Now, before you call a real estate agent or even step foot into a house, you can go online, type in a real estate company's name or real estate agent.com, and look at the homes available in a certain town or area.

There are pros and cons to this, which means, on the whole, that as long as you understand what real estate Web sites can and can't do for you, you can use them to help you both in your home search and in learning all you need to about your house, the process, and the neighborhood into which you want to move.

The first thing you should remember is that, like any expert, any one Web site isn't the end all and be all of information and knowledge. Just like information you get from a person or book, you should double check what you hear or read.

Realty Web sites are supposed to have what real estate agents have—the entire "Multiple Listing Service" or MLS, which is a list of every home that is currently on the market. The problem is that it's difficult to know where each home is in the sale process. Local real estate agents are much more likely to know exactly what is going on with a home than a national Web site does.

That doesn't mean you shouldn't use the Web sites, because you can look at local housing prices to make sure the one you're interested in is priced appropriately. You can also use an agent's Web site to find out more about her. You'll want to see that she has a few homes listed and that she has some successful sales highlighted.

There are other good ways to use the Web in your house search. First, you can learn a lot about the area you're considering moving to. You can read the local newspaper, go to the chamber of commerce Web site, and look up any tourist information to learn more about what's going on where you might live. You can read about a city's school district and even find out if a particular necessity for you (say, a movie theater, bookstore, or gourmet grocery store) is nearby.

Second, you can see how far your commute would possibly be by mapping out a route through mapquest.com, for example.

The final thing you can do on the Web is shop for a home loan. This has its good and bad elements. The good thing is that you don't have to make an appointment with someone, and if you're savvy about loans and have excellent credit, you'll be able to figure out if you're getting what you need. The bad thing is that you shouldn't apply for loans indiscriminately. In the first place, credit agencies look at—and judge—how often inquiries are made into your credit history, and the more inquiries that are made, the more it can negatively affect your score. Also, when you aren't meeting with a person, you can't explain any specifics to your situation. And, of course, you can't negotiate with your computer. You are either accepted or turned down, and there's not a lot you can do about it while sitting alone in your living room staring at a screen.

And, although you can shop online and be approved online, you can't actually close the deal online. Eventually, you're going to have to come face-to-face with the financial people and some real estate agents.

Some agents love to communicate by e-mail, others don't. Remember, agents are on the road more than they are in the office, so phones (and often their cell phones) are the best way to reach them.

With that caveat, however, here are some Web sites we've found helpful and informative, as well as reliable.

www.realestateagent.com—This is the official site of the National Association of Real Estate Agents, and every home listed for sale in any real estate office (but not For Sale by Owner homes) is on this site. You can plug in a city or town and pull up all the homes available. The site includes financial calculators and agent listings. The only problem is that sometimes houses on the site have already been sold, so if you find one in which you are interested, we recommend calling the agent right away to find out if it is still available.

www.bankrate.com—This site offers objective lists of interest rates for all types of loans, as well as calculators to help you translate the rate information to your real-life scenario. It also has well-written and informative articles on home buying and other financial issues.

www.remax.com—All of the major real estate companies have Web sites that allow you to search their listings and find an agent within their company. If you notice a "For Sale" sign in front of a house but don't have time to write down the phone number of the agent, at least remember the agent's office name so you can go to that particular Web site to get more information.

www.greatschools.net—This site is perfect for parents who are choosing between houses in different school systems or who need to relocate to a faraway town or city. It rates and describes both public and private schools. It also gives you contact information for the schools, so you can get the name of a principal or find out the names of all the schools in a district.

www.homefair.com—Another site with calculators and financial information to help you choose a loan.

http://houseandhome.msn.com—This site includes both home information (such as recipes, decorating, and the like) and home-buying information. It's very consumer-driven, so the articles are easy to read and understand.

www.realestatejournal.com—This is the *Wall Street Journal*'s Guide to Property, and it is fabulous. Designed for more upscale properties and financial issues, the writing is superb and the information is well-researched.

Lisa's Story

"A buyer should have legal representation because everyone else at the close has it."

Lisa Fischberg, Bergen County, New Jersey, real estate attorney

One of the most important things you need to know is that real estate purchasing is just incredibly specific to the laws of each state. For instance, in New York and New Jersey, you always need an attorney. The lenders almost require it and title companies will only talk to attorneys. But in Maryland and Florida, for example, it is uncommon to use a lawyer—you use a title company and they charge you to prepare the papers.

Nevertheless, I think everyone needs an attorney because every other person at the table is represented, the seller, the banks, the title company. Your attorney is going to make sure there is clear title and will explain the terms of the mortgage. Ninety percent of the time when I'm at a closing the buyers don't know how the mortgage is going to work.

The cost really varies by state; in New Jersey it's $800 to $1,000; in New York, it's closer to $1,500 to $1,800. The title company is charging you for preparing the papers without an attorney.

My thought is that if you're buying a house, in terms of the money you're taking out as a loan, the cost of getting a lawyer is not a lot percentage-wise. If you're doing this thing you should be able to budget to have someone make sure your title work is clean and that lender is being honest.

As a single woman, there are only a few things you need to know that are specific to you when you buy a house. First of all, when you buy the house, your name alone is on the title work. But if you get married, you cannot sell the house without your husband then signing the deed. Even if you break up with your husband, once you've been married and lived there, he has to sign the deed to sell.

But, if you're not married to whoever lives with you, whether it's a man or not, you really run no risk as an owner. *(continued)*

Now, a lot of people want to know what happens to the money put into the house if you sell it and you're married or if, at the time you are selling, you are getting divorced. That's a divorce issue, not a real estate issue.

In fact, many real estate issues come up during marriage or divorce, and you need to ask your divorce attorney as well as a real estate attorney about the money and the laws about purchases, sales, and resales. For example, if you're getting the house in your divorce agreement but know that you'll eventually want to sell it, most lawyers will tell you to wait to sell until the divorce is final. Although these days, because the wife getting the house is so common and because men are aware that their wives plan to sell the house, more and more husbands are waiving their rights to any part of the house even before the divorce is final.

But here's the catch: The wife thinks the husband is being generous, but then, the husband will send the final divorce papers over to her and say, "If you don't sign now, then we won't be divorced before you close on the house." In other words, it's a bargaining tactic, and it ends up getting the woman to agree to her ex-husband's stipulations in order to close on a house sale or purchase.

And if you don't agree to what he asks for before the close, then you could end up in default in a real estate contract. So, you need to be aware of the laws and issues with both of your lawyers.

Now, if you leave a property that you shared with your husband, you still own the property, and if your husband sells before you're divorced then you still have to consent to the sale.

Hiring a real estate lawyer is also a good idea if you're buying either an investment property or a place in which to retire. Although the purchasing laws are the same, i.e., you still need a title search and you still need to be aware of the repayment schedule, you should also know that some of the retirement communities have particular rules about who you can resell to, because these community property deals are really condominiums, even if you are buying a single-family home.

Finally, when you buy a house as an investment and you know you're going to sell it quickly before you actually close on it (this is called "flipping"), you need to know that lenders are becoming very suspicious of that. People sometimes accomplish flipping by filing false deeds, using names of people they know, and then increasing the price significantly in a short period of time. That can be a problem. If you see a deed for $35,000 and then the next one is for $350,000, or if a home changes hands more than once in a year, that raises red flags and can get owners or sellers into trouble. Another term for this is "seasoning."

It's perfectly legal, of course, to buy a house as an investment and to make a profit, but it isn't legal to file a false deed. Also, the government doesn't like it if you try to avoid paying capital gains tax.

There is still, in my opinion, a lot of money to be made in real estate. I have a client who used to work on Wall Street. He lives in Hoboken, just across the river from Manhattan. On April 20th, he bought a new construction condominium at the asking price, laid out about $30,000 for the mortgage. He listed the condo on craigslist.com and sold it by May 30th. He made $120,000 on the deal and never had to make a mortgage payment.

The job of real estate attorney entails a lot of research and a lot of paperwork. You can rely on your realtor for advice, but they aren't going to handle the paperwork for you. Instead a good lawyer will hold your hand during the process. When I have a client who doesn't know what to do, I tell them, "Here, do this next and then call me."

I charge my clients a flat fee, like most real estate lawyers, and I once figured out I put in about twenty-six to thirty hours for each client, which is a lot less for lawyers who get hourly fees, but sometimes I do closings that are easy and there isn't as much work involved.

I get my work through referrals from real estate brokers, and I'm on an approved attorney list for some local unions and associations. When you're looking for a lawyer, you want to use referrals. You definitely have to find someone in your own state or who is admitted to practice in your state. If you have a cousin in Missouri who offers to read the contract and if you live in another state, you have to know that the laws might be different and she'll have to be familiar with the laws that govern the purchase of your new home. ❦

Chapter 3

The Process and the Paperwork

Have you ever noticed how many commercials and advertisements there are for mortgage companies and loans? One of the most powerful things a homebuyer can realize is that she has many options when it comes to taking out a mortgage—a long-term loan that allows you to buy a home. Because homes are so expensive special loans were created to help people buy them. These loans are long-term (usually fifteen or thirty years) and involve a special payment schedule that allows the lender to make their money back (but the borrower pays a high amount of interest first). To offset the interest payments, the government has made that money tax-deductible. So, even though early on in your loan you aren't paying much of the principal, you gain a huge tax benefit for spending your money on a home.

With all of these significant considerations—principal, interest, and taxes—it's important to choose your mortgage lender and the mortgage loan itself wisely. There are many types of loans and lenders, so you need to understand the differences between them all, as well as which one would be best for you.

Well, in the end, it really all comes down to understanding how you're going to pay for your house over the years and doing what you need to do to buy the house you want, which means research, legwork, and filling out a whole lot of papers.

We figure there are two kinds of women—those who are intimidated by this financial stuff and those who aren't. If you aren't intimidated by this, congratulations. Read it all through, take notes, and start filling out the paperwork.

If, however, numbers and paperwork intimidate you, this paragraph is for you: Feel the fear and do it anyway. We could think of a number of deep and intense ways for you to examine your fear and concern, but really, who has the time? Wouldn't it be better to just go buy your house and get over your fear by having succeeded past it? Numbers and paperwork can be scary, but they are a necessary part of buying a home; there's no way around them.

Mortgage Banks

Now we're going to discuss the people who work with the numbers. These people really understand the differences between loans and what the numbers will mean over the years. We encourage you to ask them as many questions as possible, but make sure to treat them as if they are on your side. Even if they are giving you information that you don't like (such as your credit score) remember that if they are interested in helping you, they can help make the difference between thousands of dollars in your mortgage.

A mortgage bank is a direct lender; that is, bank employees alone review your application and make the decision to lend you money. Typically, the bank will sell your loan on the secondary market.

Benefits of a mortgage bank:

- **Reliability:** You probably know and trust your local mortgage bank. It is regulated by state and federal agencies and likely has strong ties with your community.
- **One-stop shopping:** You deal directly with the source of your loan.

- **Savings:** As the loan originator, a bank may save you money in the loan process and/or offer you better terms based on your total assets on deposit with the bank.
- **Speed:** A bank also may process your loan faster than other providers.

Risks of a mortgage bank:

- **Limited choice:** Mortgage bankers only offer their own programs. To comparison shop, you will need to speak with several lenders.

Mortgage Brokers

A mortgage broker is a middleman who may represent the mortgage loan products of hundreds of different lenders. The broker's goal is to match you up with the loan product that best meets your needs at the best price. Once your loan is approved, you will usually deal directly with the loan originator or their mortgage service provider.

Benefits of a mortgage broker:

- **Variety:** By shopping across a range of different programs and lenders, a mortgage broker may find a loan that is a better fit than a mortgage bank could.
- **Qualifying:** A mortgage broker can best steer you to the national or regional lenders that are most likely to accept your application based on your financial and personal information.
- **Savings:** You may get a more favorable loan rate.
- **Speed:** A broker saves you time shopping for a loan.

Risks of a mortgage broker:

- **Hidden costs:** Some mortgage brokers attempt to increase their profit by writing hidden costs into your loan. Best hedge: Know the loan process and ask questions.
- **Professional oversight:** Unlike mortgage bankers, mortgage brokers are not subject to licensing and regulation in all states.

Other Sources for Mortgages

Most financial institutions offer a limited menu of loan products just as mortgage banks do. They typically hold mortgages in their portfolios or sell them on the secondary market.

Because the mortgage lending business is so profitable, other companies and businesses have gotten into the game:

- **Homebuilders and real estate agencies**—Many large homebuilders and real estate agencies now have their own on-site mortgage companies to make it easier for customers to buy their properties. These affiliated companies may operate as mortgage banks or brokers. Of course, they will only lend money for their properties so you can't shop around with the loan they are offering.
- **Internet lenders**—Mortgage lenders have proliferated on the Internet in recent years, offering fast, easy loans at competitive rates. Some are online channels of brick-and-mortar financial institutions or mortgage brokers, others are Internet-based banks or brokers.

Which lender is right for you?

Depending on your credit history and circumstances, you may benefit by using one source of mortgage loans over another.

Q. Do you have excellent credit and easy access to financial documents? Are you a long-time employee of one company?

A. Internet lender, bank, or mortgage bank

Q. Are you self-employed? Do you prefer not to share data about income or assets with mortgage provider?

A. Mortgage broker

Q. Are you a repeat home shopper, shopping for a rate-and-term refinance, and/or financially savvy, i.e., you understand the full implications of all the loan terms?

A. Internet lender

Q. Are you looking for an ARM and have a relationship at one institution (i.e., with many accounts at that institution)?

A. Mortgage bank

Q. Are you a convenience shopper, looking for the easiest loan to get even if it costs more?

A. Homebuilder or real estate agency lender

Tips for Working with Lenders

- **Get recommendations**—Ask friends and family members for suggestions, especially if they've recently obtained a loan.
- **Check credentials**—Mortgage bankers are regulated by either your state's department of banking or division of real estate. Check with the one appropriate to your state to see if a lender is in good professional standing. Mortgage brokers may or may not be state regulated. If not, check with the local chapter of the National Association of Mortgage Brokers or the Better Business Bureau to see if their record is clean. The Library of Congress has a good index of state and local government Web sites.
- **Do your homework**—Learn about typical mortgages and ask questions when something looks amiss; a broker may be trying to pad closing costs or other fees at your expense.
- **Take care online**—There are plenty of attractive deals online, but first make sure you're dealing with a reliable broker or lender.
- **Take extra care during peak season**—Unscrupulous lenders and brokers are more apt to quote you bogus rates or slip in extra costs during peak home-buying season, in hopes you won't notice.

Conventional Mortgages

A conventional mortgage has no security guarantees other than the value of the property. A low down payment in combination with a conventional mortgage increases the risk to the lender. This is because the borrower has little invested in the property. Typically, a down payment of less than twenty percent of the property value will require private mortgage insurance (PMI). VA loans, FHA loans, and other programs guaranteed by the government do not require mortgage insurance.

FHA Loans and HUD Homes

First-time homebuyers should consider applying for an FHA loan, which is issued by the Federal Housing Administration (FHA), a subsidiary of the U.S. Department of Housing and Urban Development (HUD).

The HUD homes program is especially helpful for a first-time homebuyer with a limited income. People who qualify for the HUD homes program may be able to put down as little as three percent of the property's worth, providing they go through a HUD-approved lending agency.

FHA loans will often only work for houses that are on the lower end of the pricing scale. This is because FHA lenders want to help potential owners who need more of a boost than those who already have their 20 percent down and good credit. Also, when you use an FHA loan, you will have to pay mortgage insurance, which helps to guarantee your repayment of the loan. This can be an extra $50 to $100 a month, which adds to the cost of the loan.

No-Doc Loans

With this type of loan, you aren't supplying any documention (such as taxes, income statements, etc.) to verify your ability to repay the loan. Although you can get a loan this way, you will pay more in interest and fees, because the lender assumes you are a greater risk than other borrowers. If you are offered this type of loan, talk to your lender about what you are eligible for if you supply financial information. You do need good credit to get this loan, but that is the only type of financial reference you are offering the lender.

Fannie Mae

Fannie Mae is a publicly traded investment company that is sponsored by the federal government. Fannie Mae is the single largest supplier of home-buying funds in the United States. The company finances homebuyers, gathers mortgages together in batches, and then sells them to third parties on the secondary mortgage market.

VA Loans

VA stands for Veteran Affairs. This program began just after World War II, when the government started a program to help returning veterans buy houses. VA loans are backed by the government, which protects the lender against loss if payments are not made. A key feature is that often no down payment is required.

Low Interest Rates and Credit Scores

The best mortgage rates are reserved for borrowers with "A" credit. Actual credit scores required for "A" credit vary from lender to lender, but normally it requires a score of 720 or higher. Interest rates and risk to the lender are related. That is, the higher the risk as defined by a lower credit score, the higher the rate.

Fixed-Rate Versus Adjustable-Rate Mortgages (ARMs)

A fixed-rate loan is quite straightforward. The interest charged on the mortgage is constant for the duration of the loan. Monthly payments are a set amount and remain at that amount until the loan is paid off. These mortgages are normally amortized over a fifteen-, twenty-, or thirty-year period.

An ARM is quite different. Instead of being locked-in for the entire term of the loan, monthly payments can change quarterly or annually, fluctuating in relation to changes in the financial market. The initial interest with ARMs are lower than fixed-rate loans. This often allows borrowers to "buy more house," because they qualify to borrow more money. Of course, with an ARM the buyer also runs the risk of her monthly payments going up instead of down.

Here are some of the terms used to describe an ARM and its conditions:

- **Adjustment period**—Rates for an ARM are adjusted at set times, such as once a year. A new mortgage may have a fixed rate for the first six months, followed by adjustment periods every year.
- **Payment caps**—Caps refer to how high or low your interest payments can be. The maximum protects the borrower, and the minimum protects the lender. Caps also help guard against payments fluctuating drastically from one adjustment period to another.
- **Fully indexed rate**—ARMs are based on one of many publicly published financial indicators, for instance the U.S. thirty-year bond index. These indicators are combined with a predetermined margin that sets maximum and minimum changes to determine your interest payment for the period. Therefore if the index was set at 6.5 percent, and your mortgage margin was 2.1 percent, your fully indexed rate (the amount you pay) would be 8.6 percent.
- **Negative amortization**—It is possible for adjustments and payment caps to result in monthly payments that do not cover the interest you are being charged. If this is the case, the unpaid interest is added back into your principal.

The Convertible ARM

ARMs can have great benefits if interest is low, but many homebuyers are leery of the idea that their monthly payments may increase. A convertible ARM offers a compromise. At certain points throughout the loan, the mortgage can be converted into a fixed-rate loan, locking in an interest rate.

Lock-Ins

When you first speak to a mortgage lender or broker, they will tell you the interest rate at which they are willing to lend you the money; however, they aren't guaranteeing that rate. In other words, when you go to the closing and finalize the paperwork, it's quite possible (actually, likely) that the final interest rate at which you are borrowing the money will have changed. And, chances are, it will be higher than what you were quoted.

Borrowers became hip to this numbers game and so they began to ask mortgage lenders to "lock in" or guarantee the rate they were being quoted. Typically, when you first call a lender, they will tell you how long they can guarantee the rate they are quoting you. It might be a twenty-four-hour window, it might be thirty days.

Although we know you didn't pick up this book to read about economics, we're going to give you a short explanation on interest rates, because you shouldn't buy a house without understanding how much you're going to pay for the loan you're taking out. Interest rates and the interest program (or type of loan) that you sign up for will cost you tens of thousands—if not hundreds of thousands of dollars—throughout your lifetime, and it's important that you feel you aren't getting ripped off.

The Federal Reserve System, often referred to as the Federal Reserve or simply "the Fed," serves as the central bank of the United States. It is the government agency that prints money and oversees the banking industry. It was created by Congress to provide the nation with a safer, more flexible, and more stable monetary and financial system. Over the years, its role has evolved and expanded. Today, the Federal Reserve oversees the nation's monetary policy by influencing money and credit conditions; supervises and regulates banking institutions; and protects the credit rights of consumers.

Lenders set their interest rates at the beginning of every day, after they read the rates the Fed has set. Lenders don't like to guarantee rates for a long time (say, longer than thirty or sixty days) because interest rates change within hours. This is especially true with adjustable-rate mortgages, which fluctuate with changes within the economy. Lenders set their rates against the bonds, which are mortgage-backed securities put out by Fannie Mae and other government agencies (this way the bonds are insured by the federal government).

In general, you will have three choices: First, lenders may agree to lock in the rate you are quoted when you apply for the loan. Or, you may get the rate applicable at the time your loan is approved. Other lenders won't lock in a rate at all, and you won't find out what your interest rate is until you're at the close.

You must ask about lock-in policies, and you must ask how points and other terms are affected by this lock-in. The lender may guarantee interest rates but not points, which means the points may increase even though the lock-in doesn't.

Sometimes a lender will ask you to pay a fee to lock in your rate as well as other terms (such as points). If you pay this fee, make sure everything is included in the lock-in and that the lock-in period is long enough (say sixty days) for you to complete all of your home-buying business and paperwork. If the lock-in period expires, not only might you pay higher interest, but you'll also lose the money you paid to guarantee the lock-in.

How to Shop . . . Yes, You Need Instructions

Some women know they need black pumps, and so they head to the mall and stroll around, eyes on the shoes and nowhere else. Other women go to the mall just to kill time on a Saturday afternoon and come home with black pumps, a new purse, and an outfit, even though they didn't actually need anything that morning. And then there are women who decide they need black pumps with 2½ inch heels, all leather. They want a streamlined design and nothing clunky. They search two malls and online, but never find exactly what they want and so end up wearing their old taupe shoes with a red dress.

In other words, some of you have an exact idea of the house you want to live in, and the neighborhood or even the city and town are less important than the wood-burning stove and the bay windows. But there are others of you who want to live in a specific town, maybe even on a specific block, and as soon as a house in that neighborhood goes on the market, you'll look at it to see if it would work for you. And if it isn't exactly the home you want, you'll try to find a way to live there, because it is in the right place.

Some of you will look at six houses, while others of you will look at 100 over two years. There is no right way to do this. We are who we are and how we search for a house is very much indicative of who we are, but, having said that, there are some things you need to know when you begin your search.

First, even if you love the first house you see, or even if you weren't in the market for a house but happened upon one that seems ideal, we suggest you still do some comparison shopping in the neighborhood.

Try to find out what nearby homes are selling for and see what condition the other homes are in, too. The same people or companies build many homes in a neighborhood or development, and you can learn a lot about your future home by talking to nearby owners.

When you shop for a house, you need to balance your desires (a fireplace, a lot of land, old trees) with what each of those desires costs. That's because when a seller and a real estate agent price a home, they take into account each feature that they are offering: large homes with lots of accoutrements sell for more than small homes with fewer embellishments. Therefore, you should make a list of things you really want versus things you are willing to compromise on versus things you don't want at all. And you need to communicate these desires to the various real estate agents you talk to.

To be more specific, particulars such as fireplaces, gardens, finished basements and attics, architectural touches (wainscoting, built-in cabinetry), high-end appliances, and rooms that have been renovated all add up to more money. So, if one house seems nicer than another and then obviously costs more, you can choose to buy the less expensive house and then, further down the road, do those improvements yourself.

On the other hand, some characteristics will be your basic needs. You should know, for example, how many bedrooms you need or if you need a home office. If you have a particular hobby that requires a particular type of space, such as a garden or a workbench, then figure that in. This is going to be your home, and it should give you what you need to feel at home.

Tell the real estate agent you work with all of these things, because it is this communication that will help match the right home to your needs.

So, make a list (see "What I Want in a House" on page 212) of your desires and your needs. Here are some items to consider as well as a list of their pros and cons. We can't discuss each item's monetary value, because that will depend on a few things: location, comparison of other homes (if all homes in the neighborhood have a fireplace, for example, then it's not as much of an incentive), and its usefulness within the area. For example, a heated pool is not necessarily a benefit in Florida.

- **Pool**—Pools add value to a home, especially built-in pools, but when you're on your own, you need to remember the upkeep is costly and time-consuming. On the other hand, you'll have a ton of company if you have a nice pool.

- **Landscaping**—Good landscaping is typically very costly to put in, but the expense is minimally passed onto you, the buyer. Of course, we hope you like it, because it's more expensive to rip out and replace.
- **Perennial garden**—This is a wonderful thing, because to create and tend a perennial garden is a lot of work. You'll have to weed, but you'd probably have to do that anyway, and with a perennial garden you'll be thrilled with your home in spring and summer.
- **Older trees**—In most cases, older trees are great. They provide shade, look beautiful, and are actually worth something, because when new homes are built they usually clear-cut the land, taking out all of the trees, which means new owners must landscape. Landscaping is very expensive, and it takes a long time to wait for young trees to mature. (Old trees cost thousands of dollars.) There is one drawback: Most older trees are great, but look up and see if there are trees that need to be trimmed, if branches are hitting windows, or if heavy branches are hanging over roofs. And check the roots of the trees, too: Are there lots of exposed roots? If so, you might need to put down grass. This is something that can be used to show that you're going to need to put work into the lawn.
- **Renovated kitchen**—This is, in 99.9 percent of cases, a good thing, especially if care was taken to choose high-quality appliances and neutral colors (so you can use paint to reflect your personality rather than having to decorate around the refrigerator). The con is that you're going to have pay for this (the owner did), and many buyers will want this option, so it's not something you can really haggle over in terms of price. Also, if you don't like the renovated kitchen, there's probably not much you'll be able to do about it in the near future.
- **Renovated bathroom**—Say hallelujah! Although, of course, when a bathroom hasn't been renovated, you can use that fact to bargain the price down. Once again, there's not much you can say against a new bathroom, especially if it's been done well. The only real problem is if the current owners choose avocado green as the color scheme.
- **Finished basement**—Pro: Adds living space that has often been created with care, such as a home office, den, or kids' playroom. The con, of course, is wood paneling. Need we say more? If you see wood paneling, use that as a bargaining chip (no pun intended).
- **Finished attic**—Pro: Also adds living space and can be handled beautifully. Con: Usually there isn't one.
- **Fireplaces**—Pro: Almost everyone loves fireplaces. The con is when that fireplace is really a wood stove, which does add heat, but is also usually an eyesore in most decors.

- **Formal dining room**—This tends to add to a house's value. If it's not something you need, then you might look at houses with a combined living/dining room. Con: May stand empty if, in fact, the only day you'll use it each year is Thanksgiving.

- **Great Room**—Pro: In the South, a great room (or living room, as opposed to den) is usually a given in a well-made home, and great rooms are now offered in new homes. But, really, if you're not going to use it, why pay for it? (That's the con.)

- **Eat-in kitchen**—Pro: Most people love these now, and they often add a lot of space to kitchens. The con is that it sometimes means there isn't any other place to eat in the house, and sometimes it's nice to get away from the view of the stove.

- **Home office**—The pro here is that most everyone these days has a computer and enjoys using a comfortable work space. We can't think of a con, unless the construction is shoddy. Also, this probably means you'll have good Internet access, which is sometimes an issue with older homes.

- **Air conditioning**—Central air is a given in newer homes in almost all parts of the country, even those that, ten years ago, didn't normally need air conditioning (you can thank global warming for this). Older homes, especially those in northern parts of the country, might not have this amenity, but it's usually not something you can bargain over. If you're moving in the summer, we suggest you try ceiling fans and one-room air conditioners before you spend the money on central air.

- **Window treatments**—Although these aren't a permanent fixture in a house, many sellers offer these with the sale of the home, because they have typically been custom-made for the house and thus can't be moved (because of measurements and number of windows) to the seller's new home. In some cases, this is great; you'll have wonderful shutters and perfect shades for skylights. In other cases, you'll have drapes in colors you don't like or valences you aren't interested in having. The seller will see her offering of the window treatments as a gift and thus might come down less than you would like in price during negotiation. On the other hand, if you like them, then you might be happier with the asking price than you would have been. It's all about taste. Window treatments are expensive, though, so don't discount their value.

- **New appliances**—As we mentioned in the kitchen and bathroom, new appliances are expensive and often add to the cost of a house. Sometimes a seller won't completely renovate a kitchen or bath, but they will replace an older tub or stove with something more up-to-date. The problem, we have found, is that this type of owner (one who could live with an older kitchen or bath) won't always choose the classiest appliance option. You might want a clawfoot tub; they might choose a molded bathtub/shower combo. In this case, the seller will think they've done something good, but you, the buyer, won't see this as a selling point, so there is no way to determine the value, except to say that chances are, if it's new, it won't break soon.

How to Interpret Home Advertisements

Besides the facts about a house, a real estate agent or seller will also put some descriptive language onto their sales sheet or in their classified ad. "Needs TLC" or "move-in condition" are just two of the many phrases used to describe houses, and few buyers believe everything they hear or see about a home.

Nevertheless, there are some stock words and phrases you will hear as you go through the buying process. Understanding what these terms are supposed to be in terms of home buying will help keep you away from the type of home you don't want and steer you toward the home you do.

This knowledge will also do one more important thing: It will help you get a sense of the type of real estate agent you are dealing with. If she says a home is "updated" and you find a kitchen that has no dishwasher, or if it says "great views" and you have to stand on the toilet to see the ocean, then you know you are dealing with a real estate agent or seller who isn't exactly honest. And that's a problem. It's much better to feel that you are being treated respectfully.

With that said, here are some phrases you'll see in home descriptions. We've given a negative spin on most of the terms since it's best to view these ads with a wise (some might say cynical) eye:

- **"As Is"**—Usually this means that there is a problem with the house, but that it's going to be up to the new owner (not the seller) to fix this problem. It could be that the house is dirty or in disrepair (sometimes the previous owner has died or been unable to handle the upkeep). Or, it could mean that the house is clean and looks okay, but that the inspector will most likely find something (or the current owner is disclosing) a problem. For example, the plumbing may need updating or the electrical system isn't working. This means there is no room for you, the potential buyer, to negotiate on this issue. This doesn't mean the seller won't budge on the asking price, but it does mean the seller has already factored that into the price they set out.
- **"Bright and sunny"**—Lots of windows and usually south- or east-facing (those directions get the most light). The flip side of this could be that the home has very little

light and all of the light bulbs in the house will be turned on during your showing. Look out for this.

- **"Cute"**—Small, cottagelike, very few and small rooms.
- **"Deeded parking space"**—This means there is one parking space to a customer, so if you have two cars or if you have a lot of guests, parking could be a problem. Notice, too, that it doesn't say whether the parking space is covered or how big it is (if you have a Hummer you have to make sure the spot isn't sized for a Mini Cooper).
- **"Great views"**—Or other words such as "fantastic" or "spectacular." This could be true, and it could be the big, honest selling point of a house. Or, it could be the teaser that gets you in to see an overpriced home with one view out the bathroom window. By the way, "treetop" view means you're on the top floor of a building and you might only have views in the wintertime. Summertime foliage might actually block your views.
- **"Handyman's special"**—This usually means just what it says: The buyer should be someone who knows what he (it usually does say handyman, not handywoman) is doing. And sometimes this term means the house is actually unlivable, i.e., that it's something a contractor or builder would want to purchase, renovate, and then resell. Sometimes the ad will simply say "needs work," and it's up to you, the potential buyer, to figure out what that work is.
- **"Needs new roof or other big-ticket item"**—This term makes it seem like the owner is being very open and honest, and that is a good thing. And, in fact, she might be disclosing the truth for everyone's best interest, but it's also possible that you won't think a new roof is necessary, but that one part simply needs to be replaced. The important thing here is that the owner is alerting you to a potential problem, and you will most likely see signs of that problem (for example, water stains on the ceiling or an obviously old oil tank in the basement).
- **"Oversized lot"**—Most communities and towns have a standard-sized lot. In crowded places, most lots are small, so oversized could mean something just a few feet larger than what is typical. If an advertisement says "oversized lot," be sure to ask the real estate agent what a typical-sized lot is and how much "over" the lot you're looking at is.
- **"Recently renovated" or "just renovated"**—This can mean a couple of things, based on your interpretation. It could mean that, yes, the current owners did just renovate and you are now going to be the beneficiary of a state-of-the-art kitchen. Or, it could mean that they plan to charge you for these renovations. Or, in the worst-case scenario, it could mean that you will be charged for these renovations and that the current owner decided to do the kitchen in brushed aluminum and black slate, a contemporary look that you hate, but one that it would be difficult to change. Don't be swayed by "recently renovated" until you know whether they are renovations you

would want to live with. If you like the renovations, you can consider yourself fortunate not to have to live through the actual renovation work, which is loud and dirty.

- **"Round-the-clock security"**—This is another term that can mean a lot of things. "Round-the–clock" could imply a doorman, as well as other security measures such as a guard, or, at the other end of the spectrum, it could mean a video camera and nothing else. If security is one of your top priorities, be sure to ask about the specifics of this term.
- **"Square footage"**—Beware the square footage plot. Often the measurements offered use exterior measurements, i.e., the entire outline of the house as opposed to the total measurement of interior space. So, feel free to bring a measuring tape to your walk-through (especially the second one before you make an offer) to figure out exactly how much living space you are looking at.

The First and Second Showing

The first time you look at a house you should try to remain somewhat detached but, at the same time, listen to your feelings and instincts. Do you get a good feeling about the house? Do you notice that it has some of what you both wished for and need, such as a fireplace and a home office? But do you also notice immediate problems, such as a wood stove that you don't want or a second bedroom that is too small?

It's very rare that you will walk into a home and think it's perfect. Although that does happen and we won't tell you to discount your intuition and hunches, you should still look at the house a second time before making an official offer.

If you're really gung ho about the house, you can immediately tell the agent that you are interested, but you should say something like, "This seems to have a lot of what I need, but I'd like to come back and check it out in more detail." You can be specific about what you like, but if you notice things you don't like, you should mention those, too. The first showing is about your impressions.

When you come back for your second showing, you should bring a tape measure and maybe a digital camera. You'll want to really open every drawer; turn on the showers and sinks; flush the toilets; look at the attic and in nooks and crannies. You should consider bringing someone with you (not an inspector) who can be both objective and, perhaps, a little knowledgeable about homes. Write down anything you notice and anything your friend notices about cracks, leaks, smells, or anything loose or wobbly.

This way, when you go to write your offer letter, you can objectively discuss with your agent what price seems fair and reasonable based on your knowledge of the house that the seller has described. For example, they may say "large master bedroom," but "large" is relative and an exact measurement will help prove your point.

You're not going to bring up specifics in your offer letter (except as contingencies) but the information and details you have written down will help you formulate an objective opinion about the home.

If you feel you're discriminated against

If you're handicapped, a person of color, or, well, frankly, a single woman, you could experience housing discrimination. The law protects you from discrimination based on these factors, religion, nationality, and, in some states, sexual orientation. Some signs that you are being discriminated against include: agents refusing to show you a home, sellers telling you that you might not feel comfortable in the neighborhood, or housing prices being changed.

If you feel a real estate agent, seller, or lender is discriminating against you, you should file a report with the Department of Housing and Urban Development. To do this, call toll-free 1-800-669-9777 or write a letter with your name and address, the name and address of the person your complaint is about, the address of the house or apartment you were trying to rent or buy, the date when the incident occurred, and a short description of what happened. Send your letter to: The Office of Fair Housing and Equal Opportunity, Department of Housing and Urban Development, Room 5204, 451 Seventh St. SW, Washington, DC 20410-2000.

Multiple Offers

In most markets and with most homes, a few people might show interest in the same house, but there isn't always a rush to make an offer. However, some "hot" housing markets have more buyers than sellers, which means buyers sometimes have to rush to make an offer on a home that they like and, in a worst case scenario, actually have to make offers that are above the asking price and have large amounts of cash included (rather than a highly financed mortgage).

Sellers do not have to accept the first offer—or any offer—that is made to them. So, rushing to get in an offer in fear that other people will get one in first is not always necessary. In these types of markets, seller's agents will usually create a deadline so that all of the offers have the same shot, and the seller can read the offers and make a decision without feeling rushed herself.

Then, your problem becomes, of course, making an offer that the seller will want. When this happens, having an agent will really help, because your agent will talk to the seller's agent to kibbitz about what the seller is really looking for (a quick close, lots of up-front cash, no negotiating, or, in some cases, the nicest person who can move into the home she raised her five kids in).

But before you immediately rush into the multiple offer fever, there are a few things you need to be aware of. The first is, the agent could be bluffing or, perhaps, exaggerating. If, as far as you know, a market isn't that hot or if a home doesn't seem like it would instigate a bidding war, don't panic. Take a few days, and remember that unless a seller is in a big rush, she'll be happy to get more than a few options on her home.

Revealing that there are multiple offers is up to the seller. The buyer has no "rights" to know if there are more offers. In fact, all offers must be submitted until the seller has made a final decision, i.e., a real estate agent can't withhold any offers just because the seller is still deciding about one or more other offers.

It's now time to write the offer letter (see "Sample Offer Letter" in Part 3) and, for this, you will have your real estate agent help you. If you don't have an agent, definitely do this with a lawyer, because once your offer has been accepted, you can't rescind it unless something goes wrong in the inspection or with something mentioned in the contingencies. And, since you will put down earnest money with your letter, you'll want to make sure the terms contained within the letter are those you can live with.

The Secret Decision-Making Method

One more thing: although we are all for the notion of using your instincts and listening to your gut, we've come across a system that we use to help us make a decision. First, make a list of all the pros and cons, pros in one column, cons in another. And don't hold anything back, no matter how insignificant. Then, rate each item on a scale of importance from 1 to 20. One is not important, 20 is of utmost importance. Try to stay away from just using numbers like 5, 10, 15. Be really specific: have to paint the bathrooms right away, 6; love the greenhouse, 19; hate the lack of a lawn, 19. Now, add up the numbers in both columns. Finally, subtract the negative number from the positive number. If you end up with a negative number, then that's not the house for you. The negatives outweigh the positives.

Ideally you'll end up with a few houses with positive numbers. Chances are one or two will be significantly higher than the others. At this point, if you really stuck between two homes, put the lists away for a few days (or even an hour or so if that's all you have) and then start the process again with just the two you're choosing between. And, of course, this might be the perfect time to use your gut.

One last thing: You should definitely include financial issues in these lists. If, while you're writing down your pros and cons, you find yourself worrying about a large mortgage payment or dismissing a small condo fee in favor of a view you love, you'll be able to see those results on paper. The numbers really reflect your instincts and preferences, while the list is the practical side of the decision-making process.

I want to handle my mortgage properly. How can I be a good borrower?

Even if you've never borrowed a nickel from anyone or ever used a credit card, unless you've been gifted with a few hundred thou then chances are, you're about to borrow a large amount of dough (and if you have been gifted with a few hundred thou, chances are you aren't reading this book, but I digress).

You'll want to be a good borrower for a number of reasons. First, nothing is as important as your mortgage history when it comes to your credit history and your credit rating. Second, this is your home so if you don't handle the financial part successfully, you could lose the place where you live. Third, the better you handle a mortgage, the more likely you will be to be more financially secure as you get older.

How to Make an Offer

All offers need to be made in writing by letter. Your real estate agent will have an offer letter template (they are also available online) but, in general, you will make note of the date, home address, the price you are offering, and any stipulations you want the seller to consider (such as inspection qualifications and dates by which you need an answer). It is very important, if you don't have a real estate agent, that you have a lawyer look at your letter, because, if your offer is accepted, you are liable to stick to its terms or conditions (or the lack of them). You will also include a check as an offer of good faith. It's usually $1,000 (or more in a crowded, expensive housing market).

As we've said, the seller has asked for a certain price, but he has been told by his real estate agent and most likely understands that he's not going to get exactly what he wants. (Although, in some housing markets, the competition for a home is so intense that the seller will get more than what he's asking for. We'll discuss that situation next.)

For the most part, you'll be making an offer to the seller based on what you think the home is worth and what you can pay. And you'll be able to back up your offer with all the research you've done.

One thing you'll include is earnest money (sometimes called a good faith deposit), which is a check that you can apply to your down payment or at the close, so the seller knows you are truly serious about the deal. These days this is usually $1,000 or, more appropriately, five to ten percent of the asking price. Earnest money can be paid with loan money that you are expected to return.

Things You Can Ask For

One of the most common things to ask for is that the seller pay for all of or part of the one-time closing costs. If they do this, though, you can't expect them to drop the cost of the house as much, so it's kind of a "six of one/half a dozen of the other" situations—because if you don't ask the seller to do this, then you might be able to get away with making a lower offer on the house.

Different types of loans have different rules about what the owner can contribute to the closing costs. In traditional loans, you can only ask the seller to pay nonrecurring costs and up to 6 percent of the purchase price if you are putting down 10 percent. If you are putting down less than 10 percent, the seller can only contribute 3 percent.

If you're going to use a VA loan, you can ask the seller to pay all of the closing costs, which means you are paying no closing costs and no down payment.

If you take out an FHA loan, you can also ask the seller to pay all closing costs. However, the buyer must have a minimum 3 percent investment in the property, whether that is applied toward down payment, closing costs, or prepaids. The prepaids are fees that were mentioned earlier, such as inspection costs. The 3 percent can be from the buyer's own pocket or a gift from a family member.

How to Get an Inspection— Why a Few Hundred Dollars Can Save You Thousands in the Long Run

The house looks great and the seller has accepted your offer, but you've noticed something: Throughout the process everyone has bandied about the phrase "subject to inspection," but to you, the house is perfect, and besides, the seller and real estate agent gave you a sheet of information about the home, such as the age of the boiler and the date the roof was installed, so why do you need an inspection? Because sellers lie (sometimes) and things can change in the time between when a house is listed and a house is bought. It is up to you to use the inspection to make sure you don't buy a house with unforeseen problems, and it is also an opportunity to negotiate the terms, conditions, and costs of the house to your advantage.

And, by the way, the inspection isn't done just for your benefit. Many lenders require a certificate from a qualified inspector stating that your potential home is free from termites and other pests and pest damage, as well as a report with detailed information about other potential issues, such as asbestos and the structure of the house.

This is why your offer will most likely include a clause that allows you to have an inspection and gives you the right to terminate the agreement if you find the home isn't good enough to buy. This clause will specify the terms to which both the buyer and seller are obligated. You will want to have the home inspected within a few days after you sign the purchase agreement.

Buyers, not sellers, pay for these inspections so the inspector is working for them, not the seller. You may wish to include in your agreement of sale the right to cancel if you are not satisfied with the inspection results. You can also use the information to renegotiate for a lower sale price or require the seller to make repairs. (See sidebar on page 118.)

Plan to go to the inspection and follow the inspector around asking as many questions as possible—remember this is going to be your home and you need to understand every nook and cranny! Most inspectors will point out the areas that are potential problems, as well as aspects of the house that are in good shape. This is important because you will be able to see for yourself the extent of problems that are sometimes hard for an inspector to convey in a report. Most inspectors will also show you how the heating system works and show you what things will need to be maintained in order to keep the home in good condition.

Remember, almost all homes will show problems. Even newly constructed homes will have problems noted on an inspection report. Your inspector will be able to identify major problems that will be costly to fix. Minor problems are to be expected and can be repaired after closing. Major problems may require a negotiation between you and the seller as to how to fix them. A seller may adjust the purchase price or contract terms if major problems are found. If the problems are costly, you will be able to make a more informed decision about the house with the proper knowledge about its potential future cost.

My real estate agent has offered to give me the name of an inspector, but shouldn't I use someone who isn't connected to someone who stands to make money from this deal?

The short answer is yes, especially because it would seem to make you feel better, and that's what matters most. While it's certainly true that many real estate agents know completely reliable and trustworthy inspectors, it is also true that inspectors vary in professionalism and ability, and, in this case, you are relying on your real estate agent's judgment of another person. So, if you would feel better hiring an inspector on your own, by all means, feel free to do so. Just be sure to ask the inspector the right questions (see list on page 224) and, if the inspector does a good job, be sure to give her name to your real estate agent!

The Purpose of an Inspection

A home inspection is a checklist of items that determine the quality of a house, taking into account its age and location. Inspectors look at various aspects of the house—such as the roof and the foundation—and then write down whether that part appears to be up to code and fits what the seller has said.

The inspection report will include areas of the home's interior and exterior, from the roof to the foundation and the exterior drainage and retaining walls. An inspection will determine the areas of a home that are not performing properly, as well as items that are beyond their useful life or are unsafe. If problems or symptoms are found, the inspector may recommend further evaluation. A home inspection is not a warranty or insurance policy—there is no guarantee that problems won't develop in the future (even soon after you buy the house).

An inspection should determine the condition of the plumbing, heating, cooling, and electrical systems. The inspector will also examine the basic structure to make sure it is sound and to determine the condition of the roof, siding, windows, and doors—something few of us know how to do on our own. And he'll notice simple things that many first-time homebuyers don't realize. For example, did you know that a lot should be graded away from the house so that water does not drain toward the house and into the basement? And if a house has a sump pump in the basement, chances are it's a sign that the current owner is struggling with flooding issues.

What Happens During an Inspection?

The first step in inspecting a home is to examine the big picture. The inspector will note the home's location. Are there other homes of similar age and construction details relative to the home? A comparison will give you a general idea of the upkeep of the home. Have there been significant modifications to the exterior of the building, and if so, how is the workmanship?

Then, she will look at the exterior front of the house and work her way around the house at a distance that allows her to look at the house in a general way. On each face (front, sides, rear) she'll begin her inspection at the top of the structure and work her way down to the ground and lot area. So, she'll look at the chimneys, roof, gutters, and then move down the exterior wall coverings (brick, wood, aluminum), noting windows, doors, etc. She'll examine any porches or decks down to the foundation, then the grade or slope of the lot area, followed by any coverings, such as flower beds, walkways, interlocking brick, driveways, etc.

She will then move closer to the house to examine more closely any details she noticed on the general inspection.

Now it's time to go inside.

This inspection begins in the basement and then follows a floor-to-ceiling system throughout each floor in the house. She'll also notice any major appliances and hardware in the house. And when she sees a door, she'll open it! The inspector will look at floors, walls (and the way they join together), and then the ceiling. She'll also check out the furnace, hot water heater, electrical panel, plumbing system, etc.

In finished rooms she'll notice the floors, walls (including windows), and ceiling. Next she'll look for the heat sources, electrical outlets and switches, fireplaces, closets, etc. In bathroom and kitchen, she'll check out the plumbing fixtures.

Generally, a thorough, complete home inspection lasts between three and five hours, sometimes longer.

It's rare for a defect to stop the sale of a house (although it can happen). The reality is, most serious defects are visible to real estate agents, and they won't risk their reputation misrepresenting the condition of a home (which is why some houses are listed as fixer-uppers or as homes that need plenty of TLC). You should discuss any defect with the inspector and real estate agent.

How to Find a Reliable Inspector

Each home inspection company has its own pricing structure. Inspection fees vary based on the area of the country and the type, size, and features of the home or building. Most inspectors will charge extra for services such as radon testing, termite inspections, well, and septic inspections. A typical inspection fee for a 2,000 square foot home varies from $190 to $500 in big cities. You get what you pay for when it comes to inspectors, though, so check the inspector's credentials and compare the types of reports any two inspectors will do if they quote two very different prices.

Ask the inspector what he does for the price he quotes you, and be sure he mentions problems specific to your area, such as asbestos, termites, or roof issues in heavy rain areas. You might also want some specific testing, such as radon and water samples.

Find out how much experience an inspector has. If an inspector has not been performing inspections very long that does not mean that he or she is not qualified, it just means that you will need to ask more questions.

Has the inspector gone through any extensive training in home inspection? There are several training companies that provide hands-on training. Also, you may ask what other related experience the inspector has. Many inspectors have been in the building trades for several years and have considerable knowledge of home construction.

Does the inspector belong to a professional home inspection organization? Companies that are affiliated with professional organizations are serious about what they do, and they know about all the new developments in their fields. They are kept up-to-date about changes in the building codes and city requirements. Some of them include:

- American Society of Home Inspectors (ASHI)
- National Association of Home Inspectors (NAHI)
- National Academy of Building Inspection Engineers (NABIE)
- California Real Estate Inspection Association (CREIA)
- National Institute of Building Inspectors (NIBI)

There are several other local organizations that provide support for the home inspectors in certain states or regions. It is important that the inspector belongs to an association and abides by a set of guidelines that require professionalism in the industry.

Does the inspector carry professional liability insurance (errors and omissions insurance)? Make sure you ask for a copy of their liability insurance policy. If you ever need to collect on a legal judgment, the inspector's insurance policy will be able to pay on your claim. An inspector without insurance my not be able to pay your claim.

I love the house but the inspection revealed problems! Do I have to back out of the deal?

There is no short or easy answer to this question. (Sorry!) The answer lies in specifics: What exactly are the problems? How expensive are they? Can they even be fixed? And what will the seller do to either help fix the problems or compensate you for the expense of fixing them either before or after you move in to the house?

At this point, you need to discuss your options with the real estate agent. If you would like to go ahead with the deal, you'll probably want to bring in an expert for the specific problem (such as a plumber or contractor) to give you an estimate on the work that needs to be done. You can present this estimate to the seller for further discussion on repairs and price.

How to Negotiate

Ready to be incensed? Women pay, on average, 46 percent more for goods and products than men. And part of the reason for this is a woman's fear of negotiation. We're going to give you a generalization here: Most girls are brought up to be nice and smile in the company of strangers (and family and friends), but that really doesn't work with someone who wants to take your money. And, trust us, when mortgage lenders see a single woman approaching, they don't feel like they have to take care of you because you're alone. They know this is about money and nothing else.

So, summon your inner Martha Stewart, Hillary Clinton, or Lynne Cheney, and remember it's your money that you're protecting, not your personality. Make the decision within yourself to view the home-buying process as a negotiation even before you start to consider which aspects of your deal you want to change.

Here's a crash course in the art of negotiation.

- Recognize that everything is negotiable. Don't be afraid to ask questions about the price of everything in the contract, and pay attention to the response. See where there is wiggle room. Sometimes, when confronted, lenders will change rates or prices, but they won't do it unless you take the initiative to stand up for yourself and ask for what you believe you deserve.
- Say what you mean without wavering and don't ask for permission; instead, ask for what you want. And state it in positive, active terms framed in your needs, not in getting the other party's approval. In other words, don't say, "Would it be okay if you told me what a lender's fee is? I'm not sure I can afford that." Instead, say something like, "I don't know what this lender's fee is, and it seems like something I shouldn't have to pay. "This statement puts the other person on the defensive (which is what you want) and establishes who is in charge—you. You are. It's your money.
- Then, play hard ball, but keep the situation win/win, not win/lose. You want the loan, but you also don't want to give them more of your money than you have to. Explain what you need, back it up with a reason, and then listen to what the other person says.
- Remember, the other person might not be a great negotiator (few people are) so feel confident and stay powerful. Don't assume he (or she) is better at this than you are.
- Do your homework and don't be afraid to show it. Bring this book with you and show the lender what you've learned.

- Don't get emotional. Tears will not get you what you want. Neither will yelling. So, when you're talking to a lender or a seller (or a seller's agent) don't tell them your sob story about how you need this home. Just stick with the facts and use logic and rational thinking and discussion to make your points, because if you don't have a strong case (and your emotions are not a case in this situation) then you won't get what you want anyway. So you might as well hold your head up high.
- Don't bluff if you can't afford to lose.

Use the Title Search to Your Advantage

In the majority of title searches—in which a lawyer or title company looks to find any liens against a property—nothing comes up. However, in 25 percent of the searches, something comes up. This could be a long-lost relative who has a claim on a property, a water rights or utility issue, or an unpaid bill against the property. Or, it's possible that a neighbor may actually have rights to a section of your property that seems to belong to you but is actually part of a neighboring lot.

This may sound like the kind of irritation that won't have any actual relevance to your home purchase, but here is the potential problem: If you don't look at the title search results closely, you could have a power company come to you in five years and say they have the right to build on your property. And there may be nothing you can do about that, which means your property value would go down significantly, not to mention that you most likely don't want to share your lot with a power company.

Title search problems are tied to specific areas of the country. For example, in the West, water and mineral rights are a potential problem, while, in the East, lot boundaries often change over the years. For example, if you buy a house that has been in one family for generations and they have always allowed their back neighbors to garden on the lot, you might assume that land belongs to the people behind you. The truth is, it might be your land. A good title search will turn up that information.

In fact, it's always a good idea to walk around your property, especially if it is large, and talk to your neighbors before you buy the home. Ask them where they think the property lines are. Carry your lot descriptions with you to refer to. Don't think this is rude—your neighbors should understand that you are making a significant investment and just want to be sure you know what you are buying. In most cases, they will have done the same thing and will be happy to learn more about you—their potential new neighbor.

Title insurance is designed to protect you from events that happened in the past, such as liens and easements that you are unaware of. This differs from most other types of insurance, which is designed to protect you from events that might happen in the future. You do not have to buy title insurance, and it isn't inexpensive, averaging just a couple of hundred dollars over the life of a loan.

Your offer clause should be sure to include a provision that if the title search turns up something you didn't expect—such as a neighbor's right to use half of your backyard or a power company's potential ability to build on your lot—you can back out of the deal. Or, if you want, you might be able to use this knowledge to your advantage. Because, it may end up being you who deals with the issue, not the current owner.

Remember to read the title insurance policy carefully to find out what it will cover and what it won't. And, be sure the title insurance, the title search, and your description of the lot are one and the same. It is discrepancies in these that end up being a problem.

Buyer's Markets Versus Seller's Markets

You might have heard these expressions and wondered what they mean to you, a buyer. In real estate, supply and demand concerns available inventory and how long houses stay on the market. If there is a longer inventory time, then it's a buyer's market. Shorter inventory periods are seller's markets. Basically, it's a shortcut way of determining how much power you have in any given housing market, and it follows the law of supply and demand. When it's a "buyer's market" then available homes are plentiful and prices are relatively low because of that (the old supply and demand theory). During a "seller's market" there aren't many houses for sale and prices are up.

Some markets, such as San Francisco and New York, are almost always seller's markets, because there always seems to be a huge number of people who want to live and buy in those areas. Other markets are notoriously flat and prices don't change much over the years.

Having this information is important because if you're on the fence about whether it's the right time for you to buy a house, you might want to wait for the market to turn (if it's now a seller's market). Although, of course, you can't depend on these things to happen like clockwork.

Questions People Forget to Ask, Such as "What Are the Utility Bills?"

Surprises. They're good when they're jewelry or love at first sight, but usually bad if they fall under any other category, especially if it's something that's going to cost you money you didn't expect to spend. Here is a list of questions many buyers forget to ask—and the answers can make the difference between a house deal you feel good about and a house deal that leaves you with a bad taste in your mouth.

Remember that once you have the answers to these questions, you can use this knowledge as a bargaining chip.

Often Overlooked Question #1: How Much Are Your Typical Utility Bills?

This is an important question because you'll need to be sure you figure this cost into your monthly (or annual) budget. Heating or air-conditioning a home can be a significant expense. While some homeowners take the time (and, pardon the pun, energy) to make sure their houses are energy-efficient, not all do. And, more so, if it's up to you to turn a drafty or overheated home into a comfortable one, then you need to be aware of that before you buy the house. Adding central air or changing from oil to gas heat are all costly, and, once again, if you think you're going to make that kind of adaptation to the house, you'll want to go into the deal understanding that reality. A seller will often give you copies of the utility bills if you ask for them.

Often Overlooked Question #2: What's That Smell?

Did you walk into a house with a candle or burning incense? Many sellers use this technique to cover up the scent of an animal, and sometimes those odors are impossible to remove permanently. Try to see what that odor is masking. Open a door or window and let the scent of the candle waft outside, then sniff. If you really don't smell anything unpleasant, the candle might have been placed there just to make the place seem cozy (does it smell like apple pie?). But, if you do get a whiff of urine or wet fur, check to see if it's coming from the floor (especially under rugs) or walls.

Often Overlooked Question #3: What's the Traffic Like?

You see the house on a weekday morning and everything seems quiet, but who knows what that road is like in the evening during rush hour or on the weekends if the house is one block from the beach or right near the mall. If you are very serious about a home, drive past it a few times at different times of the day and on different days to see if there's anything you haven't yet noticed. Besides traffic, there could be noise or maybe crowds of kids who use your soon-to-be yard as a way to get to the park directly behind you. These things may not bother you, but the important thing is that you know about them so you aren't surprised after you move in.

Often Overlooked Question #4: How Are the Neighbors?

This is a tough one, because you can't be sure you'll get an honest answer from the seller and what the seller thinks of the neighbors may not be what you think. We know a woman who lived in a duplex with her young son. All the neighborhood kids played in her yard, which she loved. The woman next door to her, however, hated the noise (even though she also had a child) and moved to another, quieter, home. Some people like tight-knit communities, other people like quiet and privacy.

Here's what we advise. Ask, in a neutral tone of voice, what the neighbors are like. You might have to ask the real estate agent, who will ask the seller, who will relay the answer to you. Don't tell the real estate agent what you're looking for (companionship versus privacy, quiet versus group parties). Instead ask, "What's the neighborhood like?" Then, listen carefully for some key words, such as "close-knit" or "quiet" and see if that's what you are looking for. Be honest with yourself, too. If you really do like peace and quiet, don't think you will get used to lots of kids around or neighbors who will knock on your door for cups of sugar.

Often Overlooked Question #5: Is It Noisy at Night?

One of us once had an adorable apartment that we had looked at only in the day. At 4 A.M. on the first night we slept in our new place, a train—both the light and the horn—awakened us. And that's what happened every night for the next two years. Drive around the neighborhood within a perimeter of a few blocks, and if you see a train station or an all-night convenience store, come back at night to see what the atmosphere (and noise level) is like.

Often Overlooked Question #6: How Close Is the Nearest Grocery Store? Mall? Movie Theater?

One woman's short trip is another woman's journey. Some of us like to visit the mall every Wednesday for the sales, others of us couldn't care less if we get to see a movie in a year's time. Think about the way you live your life and what conveniences are actually necessities for you. If you like to run to a super clean, super large grocery store every day after work, then look for a home with one on the way. If you like to walk around your neighborhood after dinner without worrying about traffic then look for a home with sidewalks even if it's a little further from the shopping in the area. In the end, you don't just live in a house, you live in a neighborhood, a town, and a community, and those areas need to suit your lifestyle and your preferences for how you spend your time. Some things you might want to look for in terms of access are: gyms, movie theaters, supermarkets, malls, restaurants, drug stores, hospitals, doctor offices, train stations (if you commute), and, most important, your friends' and family's homes.

Often Overlooked Question #7:
How Much Is That Home Down the Street?
Why Are the Prices So Different?

We discussed this before a bit when we explained what comps are, but we'll repeat the information and explain another way in which you can use the answers you get. When you first look at a home, your real estate agent or the seller's real estate agent might give you a list of "comps," which are the prices of comparable properties, so that you can see why the seller and her real estate agent priced her house the way they did. So, perhaps the three-bedroom down the street sold for $350,000 while the four-bedroom with a pool sold for $420,000. This will prove to you that their asking price of $380,000 for a four-bedroom without a pool is appropriate.

But on the other hand, now that you've done your inspection and now that you've had a chance to look at lots of other houses and see the comps, you might be able to say to the seller, "I realize you're asking $380,000 for this four-bedroom, but I don't think a small bedroom without a bathroom is worth $30,000. In fact, I think I'd rather pay $375,000, which seems more reasonable."

Use the comps in the beginning of your home-buying process to see what houses are available, but use the comps at the end of the process to help you negotiate the right buying price.

part 2

Specific Situations
and Scenarios

Chapter 4

Your First Home

I'll never forget the first home I bought. It was more perfect than I could have ever dreamed of. It was a contemporary with skylights and floor to ceiling windows. It had a stone fireplace surrounded by built-in bookcases, and the master bathroom had twin sinks, which I loved. My other favorite part of the house was the ceiling fans. Because my house was in Birmingham, Alabama, the fans were necessary to keep the house cool, and I just loved the breeze they created. Sometimes I would walk around my house after my son was asleep and just revel in the fact that I actually owned my own home. I felt a connection to that house that I'd never felt to any other place I'd lived, including some killer apartments I rented in San Francisco. And then, when I got my tax refund check—well, I realized, owning a home is not only reassuring and satisfying, but it's smart, too!"

—Donna Raskin

Chances are, if you've bought this book, you already want to buy a home either because you know it will be a good investment or because you have a strong desire to put down your own roots—or a combination of both those ideas. The big issues with your first home, however, unlike other property purchases are that you tend to be less financially secure (and possibly less savvy) than other buyers and you might have some emotional concerns about living alone if you've just left your parents or your college dorm or roommates in an apartment or house.

We're going to cover the first issue—money—in very explicit detail later on in this chapter, so right now we'll discuss some questions you might have about living alone and owning a house on your own.

If you've always lived surrounded by people, whether its family or friends, then living alone is definitely something that you'll need to get used to. And we don't think you should ignore any fears or worries you have. Ignoring them won't solve them. Instead, try to be very specific about your concerns. Are you worried about safety? Loneliness? Being the only person who is responsible for the upkeep and care of a home?

Each of these concerns is valid and, at the same time, each one can be dealt with in very specific ways.

If your concern is safety, as we said before in the introduction to the book, the rate of domestic violence is far higher for women than acts of random violence, and so you are much safer living alone than you are living with someone who is violent. Of course, we'll go on the assumption that your family and your friends are all sweet and safe.

Therefore, what you're really worried about is random violence. We think that most women are concerned about extreme incidents of violence—such as someone sneaking into your home while you sleep—and we can tell you that these types of crimes are rare. Really, the best thing you can do is to protect yourself. Read the local paper, go to the local police station, ask questions: How safe is this neighborhood? Are there robberies? Are cars safe? Can a woman jog by herself without being bothered by men?

Then, ask the police officer you are talking to (and, did we mention that police officer should be a woman?) what you can do to protect yourself. Ask about locks, windows, doors, alarm systems, and, very specifically, the block you are going to live on or, if you're moving into a condominium, the security of that building.

Just as you are learning a lot about real estate in order to make an intelligent investment and home purchase, if safety is your first concern, then you need to learn more about safety in order to take care of yourself.

Now, onto potential worry number two: loneliness.

Some people can be lonely in a crowd of people, or lying next to a man, or even sitting at your family's dinner table. That kind of loneliness—when you're actually not alone but can't connect to anyone around you—is a little more existential than logistical. We are here instead to talk about loneliness as a physical and emotional state; when you live alone, loneliness is a reality. There are really no two ways about it. The truth is, when you live alone and you feel like talking to someone or having dinner with someone or having someone else get the ice cream out of the fridge for a snack, well, it can be tough because that someone, be it a friend, a husband, or your mom, just isn't there.

I've been out of my parents' house for almost twenty years, and over the years I've lived in nine cities and five states, sometimes with someone (two men over the years and a few roommates) and sometimes alone. I've learned a lot about loneliness in that time. The first thing I've learned is that you have to accept your feelings and take care of them, rather than denying them or giving yourself a hard time about them. Loneliness is real—it's not embarrassing; it just is. So, if you're lonely, you need to be a good friend (to yourself) and ask (yourself), "What would help you cope with this feeling?" Do you need to talk to someone, to see a movie, to go out dancing? Whatever it is, try to give that to yourself.

Now, comes the hard part: What if you have no one to talk to or go to the movies or dance with? This is a tough one. I know a lot of women who never do anything by themselves, and so they spend a ton of time watching TV (usually Gilmore Girls reruns) and not doing exciting things like buying themselves homes (or going out dancing). So, even though it's difficult and risky, get out of the house. If you can't get up the nerve to go to a movie alone, go out shopping (but don't spend your mortgage money) or to a big bookstore or record store. Get outside and go to the beach or to a park. Join a gym.

There are a lot of places where "alone" is actually better than "with someone."

Chances are, then, that, over time—it's usually taken me two months—my social calendar is usually filled with new friends (and new men), and I actually begin to look forward to the time I have alone in my home with my favorite music (or even my favorite Gilmore Girls *rerun).*

Over the years, I've had a lot of women say to me, "You go to the movies alone? You eat out alone?" as if they think the world was staring at me and cared about the fact that I was alone in a movie theater. It's funny, too, because the women who say these things to me are the kinds of women who haven't lived in exciting cities (like me), traveled around the world (like me), driven across the country (like me), and danced in amazing clubs with fabulously interesting men (like me).

I really believe that because I've risked and conquered loneliness, I've experienced a life that many of these women only read about in romance novels. Seriously.

—Donna Raskin

In other words, loneliness is best solved by realizing that the answer is usually found outside of your home, no matter whom you live with. Then, eventually, your home won't be lonely anymore.

And now we've come to the number three concern: How will you take care of the potential problems of a home on your own? What if the pipes burst or the roof leaks? What will you do if the electricity goes out in the middle of the night? Or you hear a noise?

What you will do is take care of yourself.

You will call a plumber or learn to do plumbing yourself. You will have the number of a handyman who can check out your roof before you call a roofer and have to pay a couple of hundred dollars just to find out your gutter has a few leaves stuck in it. You will learn where your fuse box is and how to figure out if the whole neighborhood is without power. You will learn to keep a flashlight by your bed.

And then, after you've learned to take care of yourself, step by step and little by little, you will feel good about yourself in a way that you never have before.

Our point is, no matter what your fear, there is a way to both ease your mind and solve the problem so that you can realize your dream of owning your own home. If we didn't cover a fear you have, first of all, we apologize. But, second of all, we would encourage you to tell someone your concerns and think them through clearly and with the level-headedness we discussed the issues we covered. Remember to look for solutions to the problem rather than just sitting with the worry.

Tenancy-in-Common

While this doesn't have to be particular to a first-home situation, we included this section in here because by the time a person is buying her second or third home she is most likely aware of the potential issues of any two people buying a house together. While this is a book specific to the needs of single women, this would be a good time to discuss the disadvantages of owning a home with someone, married or not. First, when you buy a house with someone, you are both equally liable and responsible for not only the cost of the house, but the taxes as well. So, even if you are a nonworking spouse in a couple, if your husband dies or if he takes off to parts unknown, as long as your name is on the deed, you have to pay the bills when they come due. In fact, just to give you a little history, before the 1960s and 1970s, if a couple divorced, the husband usually got custody of the kids simply because it was assumed that he was the only one who could actually provide from them.

The point is, even if your husband (or partner) makes more money, as long as you sign the loan, you're the person responsible for its payment. Therefore, while it's easy to think, "Oh, great, I'm sharing the burden of this load with another person," and while that is technically true, you still have to understand that you, and you alone, are ultimately responsible for the financial choices you make. You have to make sure you trust this person. If you're married, you don't even have to sign the loan, by the way, just being married makes you responsible for that person's debts.

These days, some couples are choosing not to get married, but they still make financial commitments together, such as buying homes. This is called "tenancy-in-common," and it refers to any two people (boyfriend/girlfriend, two friends, or two family members who aren't married) who purchase and live in a home together. This information is also relevant, by the way, to time-shares or friends who buy vacation homes together. Tenancy–in-common doesn't have to involve a romantic relationship or people who are going to share an apartment or house at the same time. It simply refers to people who aren't related buying a home together.

Have an attorney draw up papers outlining the TIC agreement (even if your state doesn't require it) that clearly stipulates varying percentages of ownership, defines common and private areas and shared expenses, and establishes a mutually agreed-upon course of action if a co-owner fails to abide by the agreement.

Remember that one partner can stipulate that upon his or her death ownership can transfer to anyone they choose. The other partners have no say in the choice. Keep this in mind when creating your papers so that a clause can cover any potential problems should a surprise occur.

Down Payments and a Lack of Financial History

We applaud any young woman who wants to buy a home on her own because we know that's often the second sign of financial independence and maturity. (The first sign is not getting into credit card debt.) However, we also know that there are specific issues that a young woman might need to address before she can make her dream a reality.

The first concern is a lack of credit history. You might think that creditors, i.e., mortgage lenders, would be happy to give money to someone who doesn't owe anyone money yet, but the truth is, lenders only easily entrust their money to borrowers who already have a history of repaying loans. When you're young, you haven't had time to prove yourself to be a good borrower.

It's kind of like your resume—you can't get a good job without showing that you've already had some kind of position at which you've done well.

So, the best thing you can do as a young borrower is to establish a good credit history. To do that, you actually do need to open some credit card accounts. Start with a small limit and a low interest rate if possible. (We recommend not getting a department store card, since those usually have the highest interest rates.) National lenders or a card from your local bank might work. If this is truly your first card, don't get a limit higher than a few hundred dollars. This will let you get used to the card without opening up the possibility that you will get into deep debt (in case you find out you are someone who shouldn't have credit cards).

Now, here's what you need to do: Buy a few things with your new credit card, but only buy what you can pay for when the bill comes, say, a pair of shoes (not Manolos or Jimmy Choos) or one trip to the grocery store. Then, do that a few months in a row.

You are now establishing a record of your payment history, and your good history will be reported to the credit bureau. After about six months, you can apply for and get another credit card with a higher line of credit. Do the same thing that you did with the previous card, but, once again, don't charge more than what you can afford to pay.

Now, everyone, at some time or another, uses their credit card for something that takes a few months (or more, unfortunately) to pay for—car repairs, school books, or a medical bill are all things that are worth taking care of; clothes, shoes, and vacations are not. As long as you pay at least the minimum balance, your credit history will remain clean. However, you should always try to pay more than the minimum balance, and you should also try to pay off a bill before charging more. In other words, keep your month-to-month, outstanding debt to a minimum.

If at any time your credit card company raises your interest rate (you can check this every month on your bill) or decreases your limit or contacts a credit agency, call the credit card company to see what's wrong and try to rectify the situation as soon as possible. Because most negative items will remain on your credit report for seven years, and this can really interfere with your ability to buy a home.

Remember, credit card companies want to keep you in debt, so they are going to send you offers for more cards and higher spending limits (and ridiculous reward points that mean nothing), even if you are having trouble paying your bills every month. It is up to you to take care of your debt. Remember: Your goal isn't to have more credit cards than anyone else because that would mean you probably had more debt than anyone else, too. Your goal is to have good credit and no debt. Most people only need one or two credit cards.

Your good credit is important because it will send a message to banks and mortgage lenders that you are trustworthy and can handle owning a home.

Cosigners

One option you also have is to have someone else, such as your mother, cosign your loan. When you do this, you and your mom's finances will be considered, which will make you more attractive to a lender (assuming that she has good credit and money in her pockets). However, this also makes her liable for the loan amount and, if she already owns another home or has other monthly payments, the lender will figure her credit rating and history into their mortgage offer.

Getting money from others

My boyfriend has bad credit, but he says he'll pay part of the mortgage even though I can't put him on the loan application. Is this a good idea?

Without wanting to give relationship advice, we do feel comfortable saying that, in the end, you are responsible for your mortgage, no matter what your boyfriend or anyone else promises. And if your boyfriend has bad credit, then you need to detach from the situation emotionally and think like a lender. Is he a good financial risk? If not, then it's not a good idea to rely on him for money.

Fixer-Uppers and TLC Homes

Some of us walk into homes with kitchens that haven't been upgraded since the one and only owner moved in (circa 1976) and see potential, others walk right out, thinking first of the expense of what it would take to replace that same kitchen. Even if visions of your dream kitchen dance around in your head, how can you know if you're someone who can handle the big and small needs of a fixer-upper?

Real estate agents characterize homes into three categories: move-in condition, good condition, and fixer-upper.

- **Move-in condition**—These homes are as perfect as they can be for what they are. Even though they aren't necessarily brand-new homes, they don't require any obvious renovations or redecoration. (In other words, even if you prefer the living room to be painted green, the red paint that's already on the wall isn't peeling or fading.) Also, all of the systems and appliances, like the stove, are fairly up-to-date and in good, working condition.
- **Good condition**—Good, in terms of a home's condition, refers to the structure and quality of the house, but acknowledges that the décor or design is problematic. For example, perhaps the kitchen cabinets are original to the 1950s building so they are avocado green and not only look outdated but may be scratched or nicked. The paint might be dirty or the fixtures aren't up-to-date.
- **Fixer-upper or TLC**—This can mean a lot of things, which is why you have to look very carefully at these types of homes. Some sellers and real estate agents call homes that need minor repair work fixer-uppers, while other sellers use the term loosely when they have a house on their hands that needs major renovations.

The good thing about fixer-uppers and homes that "need TLC" (which is how the listing agent will describe it) is that you can potentially offer less money than you would have if the home were in perfect condition. Also, you can, ideally, turn the home into exactly what you want. Third, if you pay the right amount for the house before the renovations, you'll be able to sell it for a profit later on.

In fact, when a mortgage lender looks at a fixer-upper they will look at the potential value of the home and what it will take to get the house to that pristine condition. Most lenders recognize that you're not just buying the house, but also taking on the expense of the work that has to be done in order to get the home to be the way it should be. The real estate appraiser will write in her report how much the home is worth now and how much she expects it to be worth once it has been improved. For this to happen, you'll have to tell the appraiser what type of work you expect to do and how long it will take. The more details you can give both the lender and appraiser about your plans, the more likely they are to work with you on helping you succeed.

One of the best reasons to buy a fixer-upper, however, is location. A home that is in disrepair in a very good neighborhood might be less money than the houses around it, but, at the same time, with an investment of time, money, and energy, that same house will be worthy of what surrounds it. Sometimes, if a house is run down in what is generally a nice location, a township will give you a tax break or credit for fixing the home. What you don't want is a house that is in disrepair and surrounded by other fixer-uppers because then the "location, location, location" formula isn't going to work to your advantage.

Therefore, all of those pros also come with potential cons. For instance, it's impossible to determine exactly how much a renovation will cost, and it's almost impossible to know exactly how long something will take. A contractor can give you estimates on these two issues, but the word estimate means different things to different people. In other words, your renovations could end up costing far more than you expected, and you will have to spend the money, because you can't live in a house with an unfinished kitchen, for example.

If you get a loan designed for a fixer-upper, the loan officer might work out a process where she advances you the money in increments as the work is being done and then, as tasks are finished, you get reimbursed. When the house is complete, you will have some equity and be able to get a new loan based on the home's new value.

Let's say, for example, you get a land loan for $125,000 and then a loan to build your home for another $125,000. Once the home is done, it is possible that the new total package seems to be worth more than what you spent. And, since the building has been completed and you've been repaying your loan responsibly, your lender might agree to a new arrangement that is a traditional home loan rather than a building loan.

By the way, painting and redecorating are not the same as renovating. You need to make sure that the house will really be worth what you are putting into it, because if you are making only cosmetic changes then the value of the house won't increase that much.

But, there is another scenario in which a fixer-upper might be a good choice: You want to do the work yourself or with a friend or family member. In this case, you have to be sure of a couple of things. First, that you are physically capable of doing the work. Electrical work and plumbing take a degree of knowledge and sophistication, and they have to pass inspections and fulfill building codes.

If you're going to rely on a friend or family member to do the work for you (or with you) you need to honestly answer these questions: Do you think they will make your renovations a priority? Do they usually finish jobs on time, and do they do those jobs with an eye toward quality that will satisfy you? We know more than a few unfortunate families who have had simmering arguments and problems over work that was supposed to be done at a certain time for a certain amount of money.

And that brings us to another very important point. If you are buying a fixer-upper to save money, you will still need money to do the work needed on the house. You can get a mortgage or loan to cover these costs, too. To do this, you will go to the bank and have the property appraised as is. The bank will discuss with you the value of the house and how much work is needed to get it to that value. So, you might get a $200,000 mortgage loan as well as a home equity of loan for $50,000 to use for repairs (for a total loan of $250,000) since similar houses in the area are worth that total amount. Or, you might take a total mortgage for $250,000 (if you are approved for that amount) and use the extra $50,000 cash (which you didn't need to buy the house) for renovations.

So, what you'll want to look for, if you decide to go forward with a fixer-upper, is, once again, a good location. As we've said, it doesn't matter how great the house is, if it's near a railroad track or convenience stores, or is in a bad neighborhood, the house won't be worth what you've put into it. Buyers (and this should include you) look for a location and a house, so even if you see something that could potentially be gorgeous, don't think it will be worth the money (and energy) you put into it if it isn't in a good location.

Second, take a piece of paper and go through the house with your inspection and your "desire" checklists. (You may need to bring an inspector along to do this, or a building contractor, but it's worth the money, because they may be able to give you some estimates of how much repairs will cost.) Now, write down everything you would want to do to this house, from painting to adding a bathroom.

Fixer-uppers require time, energy, and skill, even if those skills just involve cleaning, painting, and hauling. The rewards for your work can be significant—lots of people don't want to work that hard and are happy to sell a home that has potential. But, on the other hand, you have to be realistic about how much work you want to do and how much work you are capable of doing and what you can pay for.

With fixer-uppers, you are adding value to what is already there. Don't shy away from making great changes that will bring big profits over time. Larger bathrooms, gourmet kitchens, pools, skylights, and fireplaces are all amenities people will pay for when you sell the home.

Here are some of the best ways to add value to any property (including one you want to live in):

- Paint the exterior a neutral, pleasant color. Paint the trim a darker color. This design has been shown to be most pleasing to buyers and reassures the buyer that she won't have to repaint within a few years. A neutral color is pleasing to a greater number of people.
- Clean up the yard. This is like lipstick for a house.
- Paint the interiors white or off-white. Once again, buyers don't want to have to repaint right away and these colors are easy for everyone's furniture.
- Add shutters. Plain windows aren't attractive, while shutters add a hint of homey decoration.
- Add a fence. This is especially important in the suburbs where property lines are often unclear.
- Replace any carpeting or linoleum that is too worn, because, once again, potential buyers will see the potential expense as well as the unattractiveness.
- Fix any plumbing, and if a fixture is really scratchy or rusty, replace it. People love shiny objects.
- If anything is obviously unattractive, like a sink or lighting fixture, replace it. You don't have to replace it with an expensive object, but it should be well-designed and unobtrusive.
- Replace ugly countertops so that a kitchen or bathroom looks clean.
- Cover windows, and if any windows are broken, fix them. This is a minimum, since broken windows signal crime.
- If a room looks too boring or if you live somewhere hot, add ceiling fans.
- Add molding, which pulls a room together.

Kristin's Story:

"My mortgage is only a little more than my rent, and the tax break is amazing."

Kristin Ellison, 36, Salem, MA

I had moved to a small town in Massachusetts because of my job, which I love, but I was never sure about living there, too. So I was renting in the same town that I worked in, but I felt I needed to change because I ended up always socializing with my coworkers. Finally, when I was thirty-five, I decided that I needed to do something for me.

I hadn't saved any money up; I had credit card debt, and I thought I had to eliminate that before I bought something. So, I decided to take a class at a community college to learn how not to get fleeced. A different expert taught each class: a mortgage lender, a lawyer, and an inspector. They talked us through the process. They told us that the preapproval was meaningless and that you need a real approval. When you're looking for rates, you'll see varying numbers, but everyone's are really the same.

I actually used the teachers after class as the people who helped me buy my house.

I never got my debt down, so I tried to find a no-money-down loan. In the end, I needed 10 percent down. I had an old 401(k) and I dipped into that without penalty. You can do that if it's your first house. I wanted to be a big girl and not borrow money.

My mortgage is only a little more than my rent, and the tax break is amazing. I paid $2,000 in taxes last year, and this year I got $3,000 back.

Buying a home is like having a child. When you buy a place, people ask, "How's your home?" like it's a kid. But it doesn't feel that different from renting to me. The place I chose was perfect because of the neighborhood. It's 600 square feet with a loft, where I sleep and have my desk. It's an amazing space, two working fireplaces in a modest 600 square feet, exposed brick, and sloping hardwood floors.

(continued)

The only thing that's weird is that you can't call a landlord. My sink was leaking one day and I had to call a plumber, and it was a flat fee of $85 just to tighten a nut. Now I know it might be worth it to buy a few books or have friends you can call to help you fix little things.

If I were to give advice, I would say to buy in a town that's going through a renaissance. Plus, you gotta know that stuff may happen. I just got assessed $1,000 for refacing the brick and my condo fees are high, although that has worked out for me. I quit my gym, which I wasn't going to anyway, and that, plus a raise, gave me the money.

This is my home for as long as I'm working at this job and as long as I'm single. I don't need more space or responsibility or more cash going out of my pocket. ❦

Chapter 5

The Post-Divorce Home

No matter what the details and circumstances, a marriage breaking up is sad and complicated. Feelings are hurt, and people are usually scared and confused. It seems awful to be worried about money at a time like this, but, in fact, money is often the biggest fear women have when it comes to divorce. They are afraid of not having enough for themselves or their children; they worry about where they will live and how their lives will change.

The most important thing we can tell you is to not make any long-term decisions (especially ones that you can't get out of) in fear. It takes people a while to recover from the emotional turmoil of divorce, and making far-reaching financial decisions during that time is not always wise.

That said, however, women in the midst of a divorce or the end of a relationship often do need to make important financial decisions about their homes. The best advice we can give you to help you make a rational, wise decision is to make sure you run every decision by someone impartial, rational, and knowledgeable. This, perhaps, doesn't mean your mother or your best friend (they might be emotionally involved) or even your therapist (she might not be knowledge about real estate). And, by impartial, we also don't mean let your lawyer or real estate agent make your decisions for you (remember, they have a financial stake in your decision). Instead, try to enlist an acquaintance who you trust and who you also consider well-versed in finances and who is financially responsible. This could even be a friend of your parents'. We have found (and we've both been divorced) that sometimes a girl's best companion during these times is someone she respects but not someone with whom she wants to share all of her feelings. Of course the two things overlap at times, but it's best to remember that your immediate real estate needs don't necessarily have anything to do with your sadness at losing your husband or worrying about your romantic future.

Remember, both spouses (and, often, children) are hurt financially by divorce. The financial lifestyle and future they planned together as a married couple is ending. Now they need to decide a fair way to divide their assets and create a new financial plan for the future. They need someone who can give them financial divorce advice.

If you are the spouse who has the lower income, find out what your rights are and think carefully and clearly about what you need. If you are the spouse with the higher income, try not to act in a resentful or punishing manner—even if you are the person who was wronged emotionally in the relationship. Acting responsibly and kindly will, in the end, help you both in court and in getting on with your life. And, more than anything, it will set a good example for your children.

Should You Stay Put or Find a New Place?

In most marriages, one person earns more than the other, but they are able to do more since they are typically combining two incomes, offering more capital to improve their financial lives. When two people divorce, one person still has a higher salary than the other, and this makes the financial issues of each person potentially very different and, unfortunately, sometimes unequal. We aren't going to talk here about financial settlements, but we can tell you about the issues you need to consider in regard to your housing. When you're trying to figure out what to do about your house (or what to do next if you no longer have the house you used to have) these are some of the financial considerations you'll need to keep in mind. (We'll get into the emotional considerations in a moment.)

Of course, if your marriage was a short one and you earned equal salaries (and have no children) these issues may not come up during your divorce. If, however, you were married for a long time (five or more years) and have children, then these are issues you should be sure to cover with your lawyer, your ex, and a mediator or judge.

You need to learn and understand what your lawyer means when she tells you about the differences between personal and marital property; how to value and divide property; what share of your retirement and pension plans are rightly yours; how much alimony and child support you are entitled to and can get; whether you should keep or sell your house; what debt issues you must continue to handle; and, finally, any tax issues that might arise from your current financial arrangement and your future financial situation.

These are some of the specific topics you will need to have financial information and answers about while you're considering what to do about your house:

> **Child support**—Will you be getting money? Will you have to pay? When you work this out, discuss the potential taxes you might be responsible for based on your agreement, so that a bill doesn't surprise you at the end of the year. Think about long-terms plans for your kids, too. You might want to put a plan in place for college now, even if they are young.
>
> **Financial plans**—If you're scared about money or the changes that are coming your way, talk to your ex about what you need, and think about how long you might need help. You and he might want to develop a short-term plan as well as a long-term plan, which will help you not think catastrophically and help you think about the future.

When thinking about your long-term plans, consider any pension plans the two of you had, as well as life insurance and health benefits.

Taxes—What are the tax ramifications of the various arrangements you and your ex are making?

Cash flow—Before you sign off on anything, look at what the arrangement means to your monthly budget. This will give you an idea of what you can afford in terms of a mortgage.

Remember, your lawyer is not a financial planner or a real estate expert (except in rare cases), so don't hesitate to speak to those experts if you need some information on your new budget, managing debt, saving money, or figuring out what to do about your house. Information and answers to your questions (which are often couched as worries and fears during a stressful time) will both reassure you and help you make wise decisions for yourself and your children. You will need to make adjustments to your new lifestyle.

Credit Issues

Very often, in the midst of a divorce, bills go unpaid, credit cards are used irresponsibly (sometimes as a matter of revenge), and financial surprises are uncovered that end up looking bad on a credit report. If this happens to you, don't panic. First, get a grip on your finances. Look at the reality of the situation and figure out how you can repay bills. Second, after you've handled the situation and given yourself a few months to correct the problems, contact the creditors and the credit agencies and explain your situation. Show them that you have returned to more responsible habits. Then, ask them to fix your credit report. If they won't fix the problems immediately, stay in touch with them to be sure the corrections are made eventually.

These issues are so typical, in fact, that many credit agencies and lenders will give you the benefit of the doubt IF you have been responsible in the past and return to your responsible habits within a reasonable period, such as three or six months. Don't let stress spending or stress non-bill-paying get out of hand.

Robin's Story:

"If you leave your own house, even if you take your child, it's considered abandonment."

Robin Barbieri, 35, Rockland, Illinois

I married my husband in May 1996. He came from money and wanted to buy a home, but he didn't want to buy a starter home. He wanted a big house. So we ended up buying in an upscale town. We bought in September 1996 from a corporation that had relocated a woman quickly. We found out it was a money pit, although at first it seemed like things we could live with. It was filled with asbestos and there was a problem with the circuit breaker. We had a 110-volt and it needed to be upgraded to a 220. If we turned on a light, something would always flicker and pop. It was a fire waiting to happen.

Also, all the doors had cracks and splits. It wasn't disgusting, but it was pretty bad. My ex-husband didn't want to spend the money to fix these things, so my parents stepped in, and we also ended up spending most of the money we got for our wedding on those problems. We finally moved in during February 1997 and I got pregnant in August 1998. My children were twins in utero, but I lost a baby at five months pre-term. I knew I was getting divorced right around that time.

Then, I had Alex, and I just said to myself, I'm going to give it a year. But I left in September 1999. I went to my parents' house. I was absolutely miserable, and I later found out that if you leave your own home, even if you bring your child, it's considered abandonment.

So, I had to find a cut-throat attorney. When I went back to my house, my ex-husband had changed all the door locks. So, my father went to the bank and gave me money so I could buy clothes for my son and me.

My attorney got him out of the house, and I was able to get back in during January of the following year. A lot of times I couldn't even talk to him about anything, but we did agree on one thing: We didn't think our son should suffer. We both wanted him to be in a good neighborhood and a good school system. Also, I had found out some things about him,

(continued)

and he makes good money, so he was willing to make financial concessions so that I wouldn't talk about the things I knew.

So, we had paid $210,000 for the house, and without my knowing it, he had taken out a home equity loan to pay off his $90,000 credit card debt. So, now I had a house with a mortgage of $190,000 and a home equity loan. In the end, he had to liquidate his 401(k) in order to pay the loan off, and I took over the original mortgage.

And I had no clue how to deal with all of this, both emotionally or financially. My dad helped me in many ways more than my lawyer did because my attorney never took my emotions into account, while my dad did. I go to school so I can be something one day. I'm studying to be a special-ed teacher and I'm almost there.

My ex gives me alimony and for the first five years he has paid me enough money to cover the mortgage and pay taxes. So I was thinking I need to pay toward the mortgage as much as I can. I'm more comfortable with the house being paid.

I have a family who can help me if I need it. My father always thinks twenty years ahead. It gives me a light at the end of the tunnel. I used to get my paycheck, cash it, and get money orders, and this is how I would pay my bills. I was afraid to have a checking account. I wasn't taught. It wasn't until after I left my husband that I learned how to do this. My father really was very protective, and he thought I would always be under his wing so he didn't teach me how to take care of myself.

So, when it happened, the divorce honestly did me in. I was an emotional wreck. Now I function beautifully. I don't have pity parties. I'm not depressed. But when I was leaving, I was devastated because I married the man I loved and he ended up being a freak. For the past three years, though, I've been doing fine. I eat well, I walk all the time. I take good care of myself and my son, and I am going to school to become a special education teacher.

My parents help me financially a little bit, but I do work for my father in exchange for that money. My father has his own business—two big garages. I clean there on Saturdays. He pays me more than he would pay someone else, but that's my gas and food money.

I don't have to do this work, he doesn't ask me or expect me to, but I have to for myself. I decided to start delivering the Sunday paper because I feel like I need to be a contributor. But then I decided that if I got all As in school, I could take the summer off from work. In the end, I decided not to. I don't want to sit back. I can get a job and take my son with me. And feel as if I'm a contributing member of society.

Of course, I have family around to help me if I need it. If something happens with the water heater my brother comes in. I baby-sit his son every weekend. I'm here and I don't mind being here, and I have my son anyway. I don't hesitate to call him. We're very close-knit. I was protected in a bubble. People think I shouldn't be stressed out because I don't work. I can fix the house; I rarely buy myself clothes; we don't go on vacations. The most expensive thing I paid for was the landscaping. ❦

Patty's Story:

"Real estate can make you good money."

Patty Chorowiec, 51, Lavellete, NJ

When I was first married we were in a two-family house. The other side became available, and I paid cash to buy it. From there I refinanced it and rented out the other side. We sold that building and, in 1991, I left that house as a single woman with three kids, but with enough money for a down payment on another home.

I had put 20 percent down on a townhouse, but when it was appraised for far less than what I was paying I asked them to lower the price. The sellers wouldn't come down so I took back my deposit and bought a two-acre outrageous piece of property for $155,000. I didn't even think about how I would mow it. It was beautiful and I was so happy to be taking my children to this property with a three-car garage, a loft, a greenhouse, an apple orchard, a goldfish pond, a country farmhouse, and a pool. I converted the garage to an office and maintained the greenhouse, and the kids were happy in the pool.

It was frightening as all hell, but I needed a place to take the children, and I felt as if I could make the mortgage payment. I was in the financial planning industry before I got married and I supported him through college. Then, for three years, I was a stay-at-home mom. Scared to death. It was scariest thing I'd ever done.

I had someone in my life, and he moved in and maintained the property. From there I left to buy a new house, because I was upgrading the old house beyond the environment which means I would never make the money back once I sold. Over the years, I added a conservatory and upgraded it. I wanted to do more but there was no way it was sensible, so I sold it for $350,000.

I bought another home that was 3,000 square feet, and I added 1,000 square feet. It was breathtaking. I remarried so it was perfect for our family and grandchildren, but the marriage deteriorated.

Then, one day, I was driving down the Jersey shore; and impulsively bought a beach house for $600,000, on top of the $400,000 home I was paying for on my own. One of the houses had to go. I opted to sell the 7-bedroom suburban home and I turned the beach house into a more livable space with a master bedroom and an office.

I'm a financial planner, but a home you live in is more than an investment. However, as an investment it is a consistent hedge against inflation. Nevertheless, as an investment, it doesn't offer quick liquidity so it's not the same as having money in the bank exactly.

These days, I'm worth $2½ million in real estate, because I've bought real estate for my children, including a townhouse, and a mobile home. My daughter works for me. Real estate can make you good money. 🌿

Chapter 6

The Vacation Home

Vacation worlds—which used to range from motels near Niagara Falls to campgrounds in the Smokey Mountains to huge resorts on the Catskills to extraordinary hotels in Palm Beach, Newport, and Europe—are now more likely to be time-shares in Orlando, Palm Springs, and Vegas or family-owned cottages on the Cape or in the Pacific Northwest. Vacations—and vacation homes—are no longer a reward for the wealthy, but are instead a normal part of life for the middle-class American. Vacation homes are more affordable, taxes on vacation homes aren't prohibitive (especially since so many people now realize that real estate can actually be an investment), and more people see their vacation homes as future retirement homes.

Many vacation-home buyers make their choices around either a favorite destination or activity, so while ocean and mountain homes are always popular, you will also find vacation homes near golf courses and skiing trails, and, of course, places such as Walt Disney World.

Vacation homes do not necessarily have to be opulent, although they are clearly a status symbol. Some people also buy them near other family members, preferring to stay in an apartment or condo when they visit their kids, siblings, or parents.

The other thing about vacation homes is that key word vacation— they don't necessarily have to be full-time housing. You can do time-shares with strangers or buy property with a friend or other family member and visit on a rotating basis.

Obviously, the most important thing if you're going to have a vacation home with someone is to be sure it's someone you trust and with whom you can be honest about any problems that arise—and problems will arise. It's best that you sit down with a lawyer together to be sure both your rights are protected and that you are each clear about what you plan to do with the property. This is especially important if you can plan ahead for certain problems. For example, what if one of you wants to sell? Or what if one of you wants to move there permanently? And those are only the nondisastrous issues.

You need to divide up not just the mortgage, but also the taxes, maintenance fees, and, if you're going to rent it out, those expenses and earnings. Have an attorney draw up papers outlining the tenancy-in-common agreement (even if your state doesn't require it) that clearly outlines all of the issues that might come up, including the percentages of ownership.

Bear in mind that a partner can transfer ownership to anyone she chooses upon her death. None of her other partners has any say in the choice. It's worth considering—you may get along with a partner fine but know you won't work well with her heirs.

Before you both sign the papers, make sure you each have the freedom to walk away. In other words, one party shouldn't feel indebted to the other party or forced to go along with a purchase or agreement she isn't comfortable with.

Tax Advantages and Disadvantages

Like any other property purchase, the mortgage interest on a vacation home is tax-deductible. For this reason, second homes are one of the most common investments for those with disposable income. One interesting thing about this investment—you actually have to prove to the IRS (should they ask) that you have had fun at your home during the year and not just used it as a tax shelter (i.e., put your money in it but didn't actually visit). Your vacation home has to actually be used as a "home."

However, unlike with your primary home, with a vacation home you have an opportunity to rent out the house, which means you could end up with rental income. When you buy your place—with or without friends—you might want to look into how renting out your second home could add to—or detract from—your financial situation (unless, of course, you can't abide having strangers sleep in your home).

The IRS requires that a vacation-homeowner's personal use exceed fourteen days or 10 percent of the time it was rented, whichever length of time is greater. Suppose a taxpayer gets to use a property for four weeks. She uses it three weeks and rents it out the fourth week. Under this set of circumstances, the time-share qualifies as a second home. The time it is used for personal purposes exceeds the fourteen-day minimum. The twenty-one days she used it is also more than 10 percent of twenty-eight days.

In fact, even a time-share unit can be considered a second home and not a rental property. Because, for every ten days you rent a property, the IRS expects you to use it for personal purposes for one day.

Location, Location, Location Again

A remote cabin in the Adirondacks, 100 miles from the nearest shopping mall, or a one-bedroom pied-a-terre on the Rue Madeline in the seventeenth arrondissement—if you plan to rent out your vacation home at any point, you'll want to make sure its location suits not only you, but also a population of people who would want to stay there at the right price.

One very important thing to be aware of when you look at vacation homes is that what you see in winter may not be what you experience in summer. While you most likely are looking in an area in which you are familiar with the traffic or beach patterns (who doesn't know it actually takes the entire weekend to get out to the Hamptons?) you need to know the specifics about your block. Is yours the street everyone cuts through to avoid the traffic? Is yours the street all the kids walk along to get to the beach? In winter, your road may be quiet and calm; in summer, you may not be able to make a left turn into your driveway.

Remember, too, that if you're planning to rent your property by the week or month through the summer you might want it to be more convenient to shopping than less, or within walking distance to the beach, lake, or pond.

And guess what? A second home can have wheels or float. As long as your vacation home has sleeping, cooking, and toilet facilities, you can deduct the interest paid on your second home if it meets these requirements (and you spend the allotted time we mentioned above). In other words, your RV or boat can be a vacation home.

Renting Out Your Vacation Home

Let's just say that you are fortunate enough to own a $250,000 condo on the Gulf Coast of Alabama. Your mortgage is $2,000 a month, and you enjoy your home most weekends, sometimes even in the winter. The only time, in fact, that you aren't tempted to drive to your place is during hurricane season.

You notice a sign, one day, while you're shopping in the Piggly Wiggly, that someone is looking to rent a two-bedroom condo for the month of August. They're willing to pay $2,000. Hmmm. Should you do it?

Many people now prefer to rent condos or homes when they go away, rather than staying in hotels. And that means it's possible to actually turn your vacation home into a source of income. Of course, you can also rent out any home and become a landlord, but this is a little different—you are only going to rent the house for short periods of time and, most likely, you will work with a vacation-home real estate agent who specializes in helping homeowners and vacationers find each other.

If you're interested in learning more about how to rent out your home or condo to vacationers, we suggest going to your local chamber of commerce to find the companies who perform this service. Interview a few of the representatives. They will want to come to your house and make sure it would be hospitable for weekenders or week-long guests. They will also explain what you need to do to make sure the home has the amenities vacationers are looking for, such as towels, clean bedding, coffeemakers, easy-to-use-and-figure-out TV, computer modems or wireless systems, and access to whatever local offerings your town has, such as golf courses, swimming pools, beaches, casinos, or great shopping.

The good news is that, by doing this, it's often possible to recover most, if not all, of your expenses (i.e., your mortgage and utility bills). Even using a property manager won't (most likely) cut into your profits that much. Most homeowners pay approximately a 25 percent commission from the rental income to their property manager. In exchange, the property manager will book guests, check them in and out, and then maintain the property when you aren't there.

Of course, renting your house to strangers might seem worrisome at best and disgusting at the worst. Will your home be clean when you come back? Can you trust strangers with your dishes and in your bed? You will have to depend on your rental agent's ability to screen the quality of tenants. Be aware that your house will endure more wear and tear than if you are the only one who stays in it.

Your other option, of course, is to only rent to people you know or who are known by your friends and family. In this case, the problem becomes that you can't ever be sure that just because friends of your friends seem nice, they will know how to treat your home the way you want it treated.

And don't only speak to a real estate agent. Tax rules about the income you earn by renting out a vacation home are so complicated that it's important to talk to an accountant even before you talk to a rental agent.

Remember, too, that people (usually) want a vacation home during the most popular times of the year (summer at Northern beaches, winter in Florida). And rental markets are hottest during the winter holidays and spring break weeks, so your vacations to your vacation home will be at less-than-desirable times.

Time-shares

Time-shares are houses (or condos) sold in intervals, and each deal is different in terms of its specificity regarding time you visit, place you visit, and cost. This type of plan is more often called vacation ownership.

When you buy into a time-share, you are able to stay in a home for a specific amount of time during the year, or you get points and can stay at a number of locations using up the points you have paid for. It is equal to a partial ownership of a unit in a condominium-style building. It is possible to buy a fixed week in a guaranteed unit at the same time every year. If you buy a floating week, you must reserve the time you want. Points-based systems allow for more flexibility: shorter stays or different-size accommodations.

It is possible to purchase other people's time-shares. In fact, resales at older resorts are favored by bargain hunters looking to get into trading, and you can even find them on sites such as eBay. These are often much cheaper than time-shares in new buildings bought directly from resort developers.

Ask time-share owners in the location you are considering about conditions in general and the quality of the management company of the time-share. Discover any hidden fees and maintenance costs that you may be responsible for as you buy a time-share unit. These costs normally run a few hundred dollars per year at a minimum. Unless this time-share company readily allows trading your location, consider buying a location you can see yourself visiting every year. Find out if your time-share company allows you to accumulate unused vacation time for future use. Some locations allow sub-renting your time-share week; this can actually allow you to cover your maintenance fees and even make some extra money. People like time-shares not only because they are guaranteed vacations for life, but also because the accommodations feel more like home than a hotel, with washers and dryers, dishwashers, and sleep sofas.

Don't buy any time-share properties before inspecting them in person. Beware of aggressive sales strategies, because you might end up with a property you don't really want to visit. These people often aren't in the real estate business, but sales (which have similarities, but are very different, too). And no matter what, do not buy a time-share on the day you look at it. This purchase is enough like buying a home that you'll need to read the paperwork carefully and think about your purchase before signing on the dotted line.

Since real estate brokers usually don't list time-shares, you can check out independent time-share brokers to find them.

In 2005, an average price for a one-week time-share was $14,500, so it's not an inexpensive proposition, and that cost is not tax-deductible, as you aren't paying interest on the purchase. If you are not in the position to buy a vacation home, but like traveling every year like the rest of us, buying a time-share might be your best solution.

Nancy's Story:

"The money I make from the houses goes right back into the houses."

Nancy Griffin, 42, Orleans, MA

I worked in New York City at various corporations for twelve years, specializing in international business. I worked for Time, Inc., and then for Italian and French companies. At my last job I was a vice president for marketing, but I didn't like it. I was making more money than I ever had, but when they decided to restructure and they offered people packages to leave, I decided to accept the offer. I didn't know what I wanted to do. I was thirty-seven, and I was single.

Meanwhile, about seven years ago, my family and I were walking around Cape Cod where my mother had lived for the past twenty years. I love it here. No matter where I've lived or traveled to, when I'm on Cape Cod, it grounds me. My sister and I both lived in New York City as renters but everyone was encouraging us to buy an investment property. So, on my mother's seventy-fifth birthday, we were walking to a coffee shop when we passed this house along the way that was for sale. We called our girlfriend who was a real estate agent, and she got us an appointment. So we bought our first investment property together.

We felt like we were having heart attacks. The house was $200,000, and it had four bedrooms and three baths. It needed work, too. We would come up here on the weekends and paint. We learned how to tile. We furnished the whole thing together. Frankly, I think we had all this pent-up energy about not having our own homes and babies. Then, we took pictures, and we rented the house out for July and August in one-week increments. That's how we afforded it. Our mortgage was $1,500 a month and we were able to charge $1,800 for one week during the summer, so after 10 rental weeks, we could pay our mortgage for the entire year.

Then, we would get to be in the house for the spring, fall, and holidays. Also, it was around the corner from our mother as well as some other family, so everyone would check on the house for us.

The home appreciated quite a bit over the years and we enjoyed it for three or four summers before selling it.

Meanwhile, my life completely changed because I got laid off from my job in the city, so I decided to move up to the Cape and start a jewelry business. I traveled internationally and got different coins from all over the world and made them into necklaces and bracelets. I was a one-woman show with a Web site.

My jewelry business worked for a while, but then the euro started to increase in value, and my business wasn't as successful for that reason and a few others, such as September 11. Meanwhile, I was having dinner with a friend who was the appraiser for my first investment property. "I don't know what to do," I told him, "I'm looking for a job." Well, he had just been made manager of this real estate office, and he wondered if I'd ever thought about doing real estate. "Just try it," he told me. So I got my license and worked in real estate for a year, while I lived at my investment property. By the next year I had saved enough money, and I bought another house.

I furnished that house little by little, using my commissions to redo the floors and paint the house. I still figured I would have to rent it during the summer to pay for the mortgage. I had equity on that place pretty quickly and then I read the book *Rich Dad, Poor Dad*. I really thought about how we were raised and what my parents taught us about money.

My parents were all about paying off the mortgage rather than leveraging money to build equity. *Rich Dad, Poor Dad* teaches you how to think about money differently. You need to build more equity in your life, and I was in the perfect market at the time. So, I took the equity from my house and bought a small condo.

It was a really gutsy move, because when you're a real estate agent, you don't know when your next check is coming in. I bought the condo in May and during the summer I put all the places out for rent and stayed with my mom. Sometimes I would housesit for my friends or for people who were going on vacation.

The market was still doing well, and then I learned about a company called weneedavacation.com. It helps homeowners rent their homes directly to other people without having to pay a real estate agent commission. So, now it became my job to interview all the renters directly. I put my condo, my house, and our shared house out for rent for the summer, and I've been living with a friend.

(continued)

I'm building equity, and I don't live off the money. The money I make off the houses goes right back into the houses. I have a house bank account so when I needed a new roof or a garage door the money is there. I earn enough money for me to live off, and I always have money coming in from somewhere. Plus, I'm getting tremendous tax benefits from all of these mortgages.

Meanwhile, recently I decided to put the condo on the market. I was a little concerned about selling that piece because the market was doing very well, but everyone was talking about a real estate bubble. I bought the condo for $274,000, and my mortgage was $219,000. I sold it for $360,000.

But there's more. Since my background is in international marketing, I've been studying and working toward getting my international real estate license. I did my first part in Panama and now I am doing Rome. So my girlfriend and I are going to get our SIPS designation certification for international properties.

Now I'd like to invest abroad. The real estate investment formula isn't working the way it used to anymore in the United States, but the international market will be like Cape Cod was seven years ago. So now, my friend and I and another gentleman from the Netherlands are setting up a small international properties company, which we are investing in together. He's going to Croatia and Southern Italy and Spain. I went to Panama and held a meeting about investing over there. The market is booming. We met ambassadors and plan to bring other agents and investors there to teach them about the international real estate market. So, these days, I'm trying to bridge my old career and my new career. ❦

Chapter 7

Investment Property

As we wrote this book, it was reported that 23 percent of the homes sold were resold within six months, because the housing boom (in some markets) was creating a market for real estate as an investment. In other words, people are buying homes, both single-family and multiple-family housing, as an investment, which means they buy them and resell them for a quick profit.

When you make an investment, you are putting money into something—real estate, stock, a business, or other purchases—because you think that over time what you've bought will eventually be worth more than what you paid.

Houses began to be viewed as a very long-term secure investment because over the last twenty years or so the homes people bought in the 1950s, 1960s, 1970s, and even 1980s were—seemingly overnight— worth far more than what their owners had paid for them. If someone bought a New Jersey three-bedroom home in 1969 and sold it in 1999, they probably paid about $21,000 and sold it for $300,000. That's an incredible profit and could rarely be matched or outperformed by a stock or business. Because of that enormous return, people began looking at the real estate market as a better investment opportunity than the stock market and other, more traditional investment possibilities.

We are not investment counselors or financial advisors, so we can't advise you on whether you should put your money into real estate, especially compared to other choices; however, we can tell you the pros and cons of this investment type. We can also give you some guidance on what has worked and what you should look for when purchasing an investment property.

Investment properties are not homes in which you live for thirty years. That's a home. An investment property is a building (it could be a single-family or multiple-family home, or an apartment house, or commercial property) for which you collect rent. This rent pays for the property (giving you a payoff to your investment) and, over time, the value of the property appreciates, thereby giving you a profit in the end, adding to the money you were collecting as an owner.

Most real estate investors recommend trying to find undervalued properties (i.e., buildings where the rents aren't as high as rents in nearby buildings) or properties that are selling for less than they are worth and then offering six times the value of the complete amount of the rents. So, for example, let's say there is a duplex (two dwellings) for sale in a neighborhood where the rents are typically $2,000 a month for a home but which are currently renting for $1,200 and $1,500 a month respectively. So, potentially, a landlord could earn $4,000 a month from renting out these homes. Multiply $2,700 by twelve months for a total of $32,400. Multiply that amount by six, and you have a good estimate of what you should pay for that property.

Next you'll have to get those tenants out of the house or let them know you're raising their rents. That job is not for everyone. If the tenants aren't paying rent then you might have to serve them with eviction notices.

As you can see, being a landlord is a job, not a hobby. There are two main reasons some investment counselors or financial advisors don't recommend buying real estate. First, the money isn't liquid. You can't get to it easily if you need cash. You have to sell the property before you can get your cash back. Second, you need a fair amount of money to put down for the investment. You can't use just $1,000 (or less) to buy property. Also, once you buy something, you still have to spend money to maintain the property and handle its expenses. In other words, money will still be going out of your pocket.

There are numerous types of investment property and numerous ways you can invest. You don't have to do it alone. You can partner with someone, be a landlord, or just have an investment. You can invest in a REIT, a mutual fund whose assets are real estate properties or real estate backed, debt-based securities, i.e., mortgages.

You can also "flip" a property, which means you will not close your own deal before you actually sell the property again. So you never take title of the property. Or you can "rollover" a property. In this case you hold and handle the property as it moves from one type of zoning (such as residential) to another (such as commercial). In both cases you never take title to the property.

You can buy land, small parcels, medium parcels, large parcels, industrial properties, special purpose buildings, multi-tenant buildings, an office development, or a large building.

You'll have to look at all the paperwork from the previous owners, including the payments of the tenants. The other paperwork goes along the same lines as buying a home—you need inspections, title searches, and to write contingencies into the contract.

Why you keep having to buy more property

The thing about investing is that you can't take the money out of the real estate system without paying taxes on your profit, which is why you end up buying larger and larger properties or, at least, reinvesting your money into other properties. There are a lot of tax regulations about this, and if you plan to invest money in real estate, you should consult your financial planner to see how wise this is for you with the money you have available.

Real Estate as Retirement Planning— Reverse Mortgages

When a woman turns sixty-two, if she has a lot of equity in her home or owns it outright, she can consider taking out a reverse mortgage, which is a loan against your home that requires no repayment for as long as you live there. In other words, the lender gives you cash based on the equity you have in your home (so you don't have to sell and move to get cash for your home) and then, when you die or when you sell the home, you (or your heirs) have to repay the loan with the money from the sale of your house. The "loan" payments are therefore more properly called cash advances.

Unlike other loans where a lender checks your income to see how much you can afford to pay back each month, with a reverse mortgage, you don't have to make monthly repayments—instead you're actually getting checks. Therefore, your income generally has no bearing on getting the loan or how much the loan will be for.

There are many types of reverse mortgages, but they all have a few things in common:

- When you take out a reverse mortgage, you are the owner of your home in the same way you are with a traditional (or "forward") mortgage. So, you still have to pay your property taxes, get homeowner insurance, and make property repairs.
- When the loan is over, you or your heirs must repay all of the cash advances and interest. Lenders don't want your house as repayment, just the money plus interest they've given you.
- You can use the money you get from a reverse mortgage to pay the various fees that are charged on the loan. This is called "financing" the loan costs. The costs are added to your loan balance, and you pay them back plus interest when the loan is over.
- The amount of money you'll receive depends on how old you are and how much your home is worth. The older you are and the more your home is worth, the more cash you can get. The specific dollar amount will also depend on interest rates and closing costs, as well as the actual cost of the loan. There is a payment to the lender deducted from the money you'll receive.

Reverse mortgages are also usually "first" mortgages, which means they are the primary (if not the only) debt against your home.

If you are interested in taking out a reverse mortgage, you'll need to either pay off the old debt or, as you can sometimes do, pay off the old debt with the money you get from a reverse mortgage. This works best if you have almost paid your entire mortgage and your house has appreciated considerably. Borrowers can also pay off home debt with a lump sum advance from their reverse mortgage.

If you are struggling financially and can get government help, some state and local lending agencies will "subordinate" their loans so that you don't have to pay off your other debt before the reverse mortgage.

At the end of the loan (which, once again, happens when you either die or sell the house) the debt you owe on the reverse mortgage is equal to all of the loan advances you received (including money used to finance the loan or pay off prior debt), plus all the interest added to your loan balance. If, in the end, that amount is less than your home sells for when you pay back the loan, then you (or your heirs) keep whatever amount remains.

On the other hand, you could end up with a rising loan balance that grows equal to the value of your home. Your total debt can be more than the value of your house. However, you can never owe more than what your home is worth at the time the loan you (or your heirs) repay the loan. Because of this cap (which is part of all reverse mortgages) the lender will never be able to touch other money you or your heirs may have, such as income or other assets.

The technical term for this cap is called a "nonrecourse limit." It means that the lender does not have legal recourse to anything other than your home's value when seeking repayment of the loan.

All reverse mortgages are due and payable when the last surviving borrower dies, sells the home, or permanently moves out of the home. "Permanently" is usually considered one year, so if you move from Spokane to Phoenix or if you change your primary residence address then the loan can come due.

Reverse mortgage lenders can also require repayment at any time if you fail to pay your property taxes, fail to maintain and repair your home, or fail to keep your home insured. These are fairly standard conditions of default on any mortgage. On a reverse mortgage, however, lenders generally have the option to pay for these expenses by reducing your loan advances and using the difference to pay these obligations. This option is only available, however, if you have not already used up all your available loan funds.

Other default conditions on most home loans, including reverse mortgages, include your declaration of bankruptcy, your donation or abandonment of your home, your perpetration of fraud or misrepresentation, if a government agency needs your property for public use (for example, to build a highway), or if a government agency condemns your property (for example, for health or safety reasons).

Likewise, if you decide to rent out part or all of your home, add a new owner to your home's title, change your home's zoning classification, or take out new debt against your home, then the lender can ask for repayment or change the terms of the reverse mortgage.

After closing a reverse mortgage, you have three days to reconsider your decision. If for any reason you decide you do not want the loan, you can cancel it. But you must do this within three business days after closing. "Business days" include Saturdays, but not Sundays or legal public holidays.

If you decide to cancel, you must do it in writing, using the form provided by the lender, or by letter, fax, or telegram. It must be hand delivered, mailed, faxed, or filed with a telegraph company before midnight of the third business day. You cannot cancel by telephone or in person. It must be written.

Tax Issues

You can "invest" in real estate by buying a home that needs TLC, fixing it up, and then selling it for a profit. If you do, in fact, make a profit, then that purchase has, in a sense, been an investment. But, really, when we're talking about real estate investment, we're discussing dwellings, either residential or commercial, that you won't live in, but that you will instead rent out, refurbish and sell, or, perhaps, land that you will build on and then rent out or sell.

When you look for properties, you will see ads that look like this: "Investment Properties for Sale 2 BR / 2 BA Two-family unit apartment. Currently rented at $475.00 each unit. Could be higher. Long-term tenants. Down unit tenant HUD section 8. BOTH tenants want to continue residing in units. MUST SELL, property in foreclosure." Your job at this point is to determine how much the property is worth right now and how much it could bring in if managed properly.

Now, you can't find investment properties in the same place that you find a home. Traditional residential real estate agents do not show these listings. You'll need to find agents who specialize in these properties, or even look in the newspaper under "Investment Opportunities."

If you think you might want to invest in real estate, we suggest that you don't just jump into a situation, such as buying a fixer-upper or putting money into an REIT, because knowledgeable investors understand what the consequences of their deal are.

There are real estate agents who specialize in these types of deals, so the best thing you can do is talk to them (more than one, of course, because investing is, at the very least, a part-time job) to find out what types of deals are working in your area, what properties are available, and, perhaps, who the other people are in your area who are also investing.

At the same time, you'll want to speak to your financial planner about what types of investment would work best for you. Do you need a reliable second income? Perhaps you would do best with a rental property. Do you need a long-term investment that might, in thirty years, be saleable and give back to you a large amount of cash for your retirement? Or, do you need something with a quick turnaround and the potential for a good-sized amount of cash quickly? Perhaps, then, you want to buy and renovate a home to sell as soon as it's finished.

The issue with buying and selling properties quickly is what's known as the 1031 exchange. In a 1031 exchange, which is sometimes also called a property flop, investors who have recently sold a property have forty-five days to identify three potential replacement properties and a 180-day period, which runs simultaneously, to close on another purchase. Exchangers must reinvest all proceeds from the sale of their first property, while a third-party intermediary, also known as an accommodator, must hold the monies in trust.

To avoid capital gains taxes, the equity held by the investor in the new property must equal or exceed the equity held in the previously owned property. Exchanges can range from a simple two-property swap to a multi-property deal that involves construction or even other people joining in the deal. Investors can also do what is called a "reverse exchange," where they buy the replacement before selling the exchange property.

Without 1031 exchanges, any real estate buyer can be hit with a huge tax bill, whether it's on their home or an investment property. The minimum federal tax on capital gains (an IRS term for profit) is now 15 percent. Capital gains taxes are designed to encourage long-term investing, so if you take your money out of an investment situation (such as 401(k) or real estate), you pay high taxes on the money you've earned.

Another common form of investment also requires understanding and attention to tax laws. Many investors these days will buy a large property and convert it to condos, but lenders know that these projects come with risks. Condo conversion loans have an element of construction/renovation risk, and the properties do not always generate a reliable cash flow. The condo market can be a little more unpredictable than the housing market.

Do You Need a Staff?

Any investment requires, if not a full-time team of people, at least advisors who can make sure that you are making good financial and legal decisions. But with real estate, you are dealing with two things besides money and the law: a physical property and people.

At the very minimum, you will need to have a real estate agent and a lawyer around to help you with property purchases. You might also consider having a financial planner who is familiar with real estate investments and who, perhaps, knows other investors who are looking to buy a property.

If you want to make a big investment that requires more money than you have available, you can join with other people to buy a property together. You don't have to invest with your friends or family, which can lead to its own issues. To learn more about this, find a financial planner who specializes in this type of investing. These specialists often have a CCIM designation, which means they've done extra course work in investment analysis, tax planning, and financial structuring in investment real estate. A CCIM is a certified member of the Commercial Investment Real Estate Institute (CIREI).

You might also want a property manager or superintendent. Property managers are hired by the building owners and paid monthly to maintain the property, taking care of snow removal, garbage, etc. They also handle the utility bills for the common spaces and maintain the property's budget. They also oversee any projects that need to be done. If they actually do the repairs, there is often a separate fee for that work.

One thing a potential owner of a commercial property needs to do is look at the vacancy rates of the properties you are interested in. For example, investors are usually looking for properties that are either functioning well so they can take over with a relative guarantee of what their return will be, or they can invest in something with potential. You might find a good property with a present owner who has poor property management as well as asset management skills.

With any investment, the important question isn't what you want to do, but whether your investment gives you the return that makes it worth getting involved with the property. You'll want to look at the length of time it will take to get your return back. What will happen if you turn the property around in one year? What will happen if you refinance at the end of your first year and hold the property? You should do calculations like this (with or without your financial planner) for years one through five, at least.

Then, you'll need to ask yourself how much you can afford to pay for the property if you are aiming for a specific after-tax return on your investment.

Will This Investment Be a Full-Time Job?

The short answer is, if you let it—and you want it to—it might. We're only saying this to warn you that many women become more involved in investments, or even become real estate agents, because they make their own hours and can work for themselves.

In fact, one of the claims many real estate gurus make is that you can work part-time and make full-time money, but the reality is that most people do not become millionaires by working part-time in real estate investment. The experts who sell these kits, along with most of the people who buy the infomercial kits or foreclosure lists or even simply one rental property, become millionaires. However, most of the "experts" who make these claims, according to the real estate industry, are actually marketers who offer some very solid basics, but the number of people who can do what they propose is very small—because they make it sound so much easier than it is. It takes time and commitment to buy property with no money down (or some other creative financing method) and flip it later on for a profit.

It takes a lot of time to go through the home-finding process, get loan approval, handle the paperwork, and consult with lawyers. According to one investor, "It took two to three hours a day, not including weekend travel time and unexpected snafus. I found it impossible to do with a full-time job. It's not the principles that are flawed, but that the simplicity and ease are overstated."

And, more than that, if you own a rental property, you could potentially always be on call for leaks, power outages, and other disasters that befall your tenants.

Bev's Story:

"I can make more this way than just keeping the money in my pension plan."

Bev Parker, 62, Summit, New Jersey

I buy properties during preconstruction sales so that I get them at a lower price. My overall scheme, which you might call an assumption, is that once the house or condo is built, the price will go up. That's because building costs go up for labor and supplies and because the community I buy in is desirable and it becomes even more so once the construction is complete.

Most people don't want to be bothered to buy a home that isn't finished and to wait out the process, so to me, this is a way of gambling. I'm taking money out of the bank or, in this case, usually out of my pension plan, and putting it into a real estate venture. I'm never going to live in the places I buy.

So, like any buyer, I usually pay a down payment of 20 percent. I've bought townhouses and condos, so sometimes I'm buying land and the plan, sometimes I'm just buying the condo, which, at the time I purchase it, is just a building plan. I don't have to close the deal until the house is built, and so my down payment money sits there. I don't have to keep writing checks. Then, in the end, the construction costs aren't being passed off onto me, but to the people who buy after me because then the price of the house is higher than when I bought.

Right now I own three different places and I bought each one for different reasons.

The first one is in central New Jersey, and it has an enormous clubhouse, so people are buying into it for a lifestyle. I like to tell people it's New Jersey's answer to Florida. I already know people who live there. The whole community has six condo buildings and 700 single-family homes.

It's a perfect community for someone over fifty-five who wants to have a lifestyle where they belong to a gym and have lots of group activities available to them. I know a lot of people who live this way

(continued)

now. My friends are all over sixty-five at this point, and most of them are retired. They're all downsizing, and yet they can leave these homes and go to Florida to have a second home during the winter. I don't want to live this way, but I know a lot of people who do, which is why I knew I'd make money.

The average community going up now in New Jersey is very large. The condo I bought was $290,000, and I plan to sell it for $340,000 or more. I could never get that kind of money in the bank or even in my pension, which is where I got my down payment.

The other option I have is to rent out what I bought and to keep it as an ongoing investment property. That would help my taxes.

I already have two other properties, so the profit I earn if I do sell will go toward the others. I'll reinvest it in those properties before the settlement dates so I don't have to pay the taxes. Well, actually, that's the ideal plan. The problem with construction is that there are always so many delays. This place has been delayed nine months, and one of the other places I own will be a year late.

And I've run into another problem. In this particular case, the builder wants to get out of the whole deal, so he's offering these amazing incentives for the next phase of building. Now, it pays for someone to go to the builder and not me for their place, even though my place is finished. I didn't expect the competition to come from the builder. I lowered the price to compete with him. So I'm having a problem selling it, and I had to write a mortgage check. So you have to know that you may not get rid of it right away.

Once it sells, I'll have to redeposit that money or reinvest in a house within a year. Or, if it's renting then, I won't have a problem. And I can't take this profit and put it into the house I live in. Also, with retirement or adult communities, you have to be fifty-five or over to buy.

Now, I also own a place in Florida with my brother, and that has worked out very well. It's inland, not on the water, and it's going to be in a planned community with an overall plan of ten years with stores, condos, townhouses, and singles. They are building lakes and schools. The singles cost $500,000 and go into the millions, but I bought a preconstruction townhouse. To buy in Florida during the building phase is much cheaper than in New Jersey. And, after the hurricanes last year, people are moving inland.

All together I've invested $70,000, which is about a quarter of my retirement money, so it is a risk. But I believe in taking risks even with money. I took the money out of my pension, a 403(B), and I'm choosing to pay it back, because I don't want to just spend the money I end up making. That would be a waste of my intentions. I have to pay interest but it's very little because I'm borrowing the money from myself.

Even when I retire, I'll take out a mortgage, rather than buy a house with cash, because I have a friends who paid for a house in cash and when it came time to do taxes they needed a deduction and then had to take a loan to pay their tax bill.

It's funny, I have a friend who grew up very well, not like me—my family had no money, and my parents never owned a home. My friend was middle-class, and her family lived in their own house. She had her own car. I always worked. In fact, my father forged my working papers when I was thirteen (he said I was fourteen) so I could get a job and give my parents money. I had to give my mother 10 percent of everything I earned. The day I got married, I got a bill from them.

But, in the end, the weirdest thing is of all my friends, I am the only person who has a pension, and my pension is really good. I've earned money in my life, invested in my life, and saved money. My real estate investments have worked for me in the past. I once had an apartment that I rented out, and I used that money to send one of my kids to college. I had to pay taxes on it when I sold it, but it was still income for a necessary expense. 🌾

Lori's Story:

"I want something that, from the day I buy it, I know it's worth more."

Lori Bashour, 45, real estate investor, western Massachusetts

I spent about twelve years in my husband's business and eventually decided I couldn't work with him anymore. I took a one-year sabbatical while he started options trading. He was pretty successful, but it freaked me out because I had an ex-boyfriend who had lost money in the stock market. It made me feel very insecure. Meanwhile, I had been looking to invest in something solid like real estate, which my husband saw as a risk. So he bought me the Carleton Sheets tapes that he saw on TV, and before I had finished chapter 1, my brother and I had purchased a property in Boston.

I partnered with my brother because I didn't want to deal with tenant phone calls and having to show the apartments that needed to be rented. But we also had another partner, because, typically, if you're buying a $500,000 building you need $100,000 cash for the down payment. I had $30,000 and my brother refinanced his condo, so we found an attorney who would lend us money at 15 percent interest in return for interest-only payments. So, in a sense, the attorney became our partner. In this type of deal, the partner gets the interest-only payments for a minimum of six months and then they get the principal back when the other buyers refinance the house.

The Numbers

The money stuff comes easily to me, and Carleton Sheets explains it all really clearly. You just need to know that if the property has a positive cash flow and you can get it with a little money down, then it's a good deal. If you can double your down payment within a year then that's great. You want to buy a property in a market that is undervalued.

So, let's say if you're in the middle of Boston or another highly valued market, you might have to look harder to find a seller who is unaware of the market, and you're looking for a property that is an investment so it has income. I've never had to evict people to make a profit, but we did once buy a property for which we said we wanted the building vacant. We didn't have to have a relationship with the people who had to move so I wasn't upset about asking them to leave.

Also, I don't fix up these places. We fixed up something once, and I hated it. I found out that I didn't like hiring contractors and dealing with them everyday. I got frustrated. So, you have to learn about yourself and what you're good at. I'm really good at transactions and picking the thing to buy and picking the thing to sell. So, I have to have a partner who can do the rents and fix things. I'm a transaction-based kind of person. I don't do well with the people or with holding something for a long time.

I decided I'd rather buy and sell quickly. I think it's fun to go to banks and try to put the deal together. I like finding the bank or the mortgage broker or the private owner who can help finance something. In fact, almost all of these deals nearly fell apart at the end, and I always found a way to make the deals happen.

For example, on the very first one I was going to lose the deposit if I didn't close the deal. I was in the basement crying hysterically, and I was screaming at this mortgage administrator. Then I was thinking, "She's the only one who can save my butt. I have to chill on my attitude and my anger," so I called her back and I said, "I'm really sorry, and you're the only one who can help me. Tell me what you need." I realized I had to take a different approach, so I started treating her like my best friend, and the deal worked out. Something like this has happened almost every time, even the last time, when I was negotiating for a strip mall.

Once You Start, You Have to Become Donald Trump

Of course, I didn't start out thinking I was going to own a strip mall. But, the government has a structure in place in which you have to be Donald Trump in a way. With the first property I bought, I made $2,000 a month, and it paid my kid's school fees, so I thought, "I'm never selling this property." But then, a buyer offered me $960,000 for it. I took the profit and figured I would now pay $400,000 for a building, which would allow me to make $4,000 a month, but if I'd done that, I would have had to pay 30 percent tax on the profit. But you

(continued)

can defer your tax by purchasing another property, but you can't buy for less than what you sold and you can't pay less than your mortgage. So, I had to buy a million-dollar property.

Of course, not everyone decides to handle this part of the sale this way. And, if you have partners, at the end you can divide which portion is yours and you can choose to do different things at this point.

So, that's how I ended up with a strip mall. The minute I rent one more space it's worth a million dollars. I'm going to sell it in a couple of years. I'm not going to have it for thirty years. It's an investment. But the management is fun in commercial property.

Number and math concepts are easy for me. You can take a spreadsheet and just plug the numbers in. You don't have to be good at math formulas. There's nothing complicated. It's really simple math, and it's like doing your checkbook. If you can do that, you can do real estate. You have to use intuition, but not emotion.

The numbers have to work. And I have my other criteria. I don't want to buy something ugly. If I get a negative feeling I don't buy it. As a reference, I recommend *The Complete Guide to Buying and Selling Apartment Buildings* by Steve Berges. I think the tapes are better. They require you to take an eight-hour day and go through a notebook and do the exercises . . . you make a phone call to the seller and you just do it. If you skip a step, then you've messed up and things won't turn out right. Remember, anything you don't understand you don't need.

Separating the Personal from the Investment

Now, these types of loans, such as interest-only, are what I use for an investment property. We live in a modest home, and our cars are paid for. We live a simple money principle in our personal lives and our home isn't an investment.

In fact, I think emotions can be a problem when it comes to investment properties. I've only bought one property that loses money. We bought an inn because we loved it and we thought my husband could use it for his business. So, it wasn't a real estate investment, it was a business, and our business was in the building, and suddenly I was an innkeeper. We've lost $40,000 a year for five years. The other properties are covering it and when we sell it, we'll get some of it back and then some.

But it was through this trauma and this fog that we realized we had some passion and ego attached to this house, so we couldn't see the writing on the wall. To fix the problem, I hired this consultant to coach me for a year. She helped me see that I'm a transaction-based person and helped me get clear that I need to sell the inn.

I learned through this process not to buy a business. Buying a business isn't the same as buying real estate. Running a business isn't the same thing as making an investment.

Hiring mentors and hiring coaches is a good idea. I'm a big fan of that. I pay people by the hour to coach us because you have to be willing to invest in yourself. We don't have any employees, though. In Boston we have a property manager. No one is on salary; a manager gets 10 percent of the rent. Or they're a partner. I also stink at having employees. I don't speculate.

You need to get really clear about what you do and what you don't do.

Clear Up Your Issues

Now, I started this whole thing for $200 through an infomercial. I figured I spend that just going out to dinner and that I had nothing to lose. I had just done a lot of work on money issues and was also totally buying into living a simpler life and not needing a lot of material things in life. I followed the Joe Dominquez tapes, "Your Money or Your Life," so I understood money in a real way, not in an MBA way. I was clear about how money worked in my daily life, and I had lost my attachment to making money at what I loved.

And that had happened because of a wake-up call. I'm fifteen years younger than my husband and I always felt like he was always too cheap, so I was always yelling at him. Suddenly, I thought, "I'm always yelling at him, and he has money and I don't."

So I started listening to him and started doing tapes. You can't do this investment thing without first understanding your relationship with money and building your self-confidence so that you know you're going to make money. Or you're just going to sabotage it anyway.

After all of that work, I was able to do things without being so pessimistic. For example, there was a nine-family property here in Berkshire County that was selling for $119,000. People weren't calling

(continued)

because they thought something must be wrong. But, even without looking at the property, I calculated out the rents you could get and figured it would still make money. So, without looking at it, I knew I wanted the property. Someone was looking at it at 10 A.M., so I looked at it at 9:30. I offered him full price right then and there on the spot. And other people viewing it offered more money, and the real estate agent just decided the owner should sell it to me. I bought it and signed the contract while my husband was out of town.

Now, in 2005, we have two four-family houses, a strip mall, a condo in Boston, a place in Newport, and a nine-family apartment house, plus the inn that we're starting to sell. I actually want to get it down to less: Bigger properties and fewer of them.

After the mortgages, I'm worth two million dollars. ❧

Chapter 8

Buying Land and Building a Home

Maybe you're a woman who has always had a vision of the home she wants—high ceilings, a romantic bathroom with a clawfoot tub, and, most important, a view of the lake. So, you've driven by the lake to see if any properties are available, and there's nothing, except . . . a piece of property. And it's beautiful. And you can afford it . . . but . . . how much would it cost to build a house? How long would it take? Why doesn't everyone do this so they, too, can build the house of their dreams? And how will you know you won't get ripped off?

Now, before we get into the details of buying a home that you have to build, we want to explain the differences between having an architect design a home you want and buying a home that hasn't yet been built, but that already has a design plan in place and only requires you to make specific requests to the builder, such as adding on a garage or a home office.

New homes can be custom-built, architect-designed, or, simply, part of planned unit developments in which entire neighborhoods of new homes have sprung up miraculously over night with little input from the people who will eventually live in those houses.

Here are the types of new homes you can choose from:

- **Architect-designed**—This would be something personal to you. You hire an architect who might have rough plans that she would adjust to your specifications or, you might have her design something one-of-a-kind. Usually you would choose a piece of land either before or with the architect to make sure the house is perfectly situated on the property. This is an expensive proposition, both financially and time-wise, but it is an extraordinarily rewarding achievement. If you have a vision of exactly the home you want, you should at least look into this option, if only to see how much your dream would cost and whether it will ever be a possibility for you.
- **Custom-Built**—When you buy a home in a new development, you can purchase your home when it is still in the planning stage. This allows you to tell the builder about changes you would like to see in her plans, such as an extra bedroom or fewer garage stalls. This is considered a custom-built home, because the builder is customizing the plan to your specifications.

People like newer homes because the rooms are generally larger and there are usually more bathrooms in the home. New homes are often more expensive because of impact fees, which townships charge to developers for the cost of hooking up sewers, electricity, and other neighborhood necessities.

Some buyers don't like new homes because the neighborhoods that the homes are built in are as new as the homes, which means there are often no old-growth trees (if there are any trees at all) and they can be far from shopping and schools.

Like any home-buying process, if you choose to design your own home or buy a new home, you will work with a team of people. In this case, however, you will add architects, contractors, and other specialists on top of your already lengthy list of people. Don't worry, we'll explain what each of these people do later on.

Why Everyone Says, "Don't Do It!"

First of all, people may say, "Don't do it," but the reality is that in the United States, about a third of all buyers—around 35 percent—purchase new homes rather than homes that have been lived in by previous owners. In some cases, the new owners won't have had any input in the design or building of the house, but in most cases, the buyer will have had at least some choice in materials or room layout.

The main reason people say, "Don't do it!" is because of cost overruns or unexpected expenses. New homes and custom-designed homes are more expensive than older homes in general, but when surprise costs come up, owners have little choice but to come up with the money—abandoning the project isn't really an option, as most owners will have already taken out construction loans and, possibly, mortgages.

When you make an offer on a home that hasn't yet been built, you have to sit with the builder and agent to figure out the cost of all the options you want. Statistics vary, but it seems that a person who buys a home that hasn't yet been built will spend up to 30 percent more than the first price they were quoted on options. And, in fact, if the developer hands you a contract, rest assured that it will be one that is biased toward him (or her). Be sure to have a real estate attorney look it over, and make any changes she suggests. Although the developer will no doubt agree to only some of these changes, it is your right both to ask for what you want and to protect yourself from a builder or developer who might be a problem later on down the line. Your real estate attorney will be able to decipher the legalese that will be in the contract and point out the areas that could leave the builder or developer off the hook over time.

Another issue some people have with new homes is that, as with new cars, once you've moved in, it's no longer a new house. Nevertheless, a newly built house will rarely lose its value and, typically, they do appreciate faster than other homes, even though new houses cost more than older homes of the same size and in relatively the same location (i.e., the same town or neighborhood).

It's very important to know a lot about your builder and the developer when you purchase a new home, because home construction is a risky business. If they aren't knowledgeable about the building business, developers can run out of money before houses are finished, or they can find that the houses have problems or aren't priced right, which means they may not sell. When these things happen, the lenders take over the buildings and their values decrease significantly. Or the homes won't be built the way you had thought they would be.

You should know, too, that you can bring a real estate agent to represent you when you look at construction or new homes. The seller, i.e., the builder or developer, will pay the commission, and you will be able to benefit from the real estate agent's negotiation skills and inside knowledge of how the sales process is going for the particular neighborhood.

By the way, you can also use an outside inspector to check out your home as the building goes on. You want your inspector to look at the house when the foundation is poured; after the framing is done; after the house has been wired and the plumbing is done; and then just before the walls are closed. And, of course, you'll do a final walk through after the house is completely finished. This way you can make sure the building is constructed the way you want it to be and that any extras or amenities you paid for have been done properly.

Here is a typical spec sheet, which explains what you are paying for and what you expect from the builder:

Raskin/Hawthorne Ltd.
Building Specifications
Revision Date 05/2005

Foundation:
8" poured concrete with anchor bolts or straps.
Basement floor to be poured concrete with wire mesh.
Waterproofing to include exterior concrete walls painted, water plug tie holes, and an exterior perimeter drain of 4" perforated pipelaid in stone.

Wood Walls:
Exterior: 2×6 #2 or better studs @16" oc. with 6" fiberglass insulation (R-19) between.
Interior walls: 2×4 #2 or better @16" oc. except as needed for plumbing.

Interior finish: 4 mill poly on exterior walls, 1/2" drywall, typical finish with spray/texture ceiling finish/wall primer coat.
Garage drywall to be per code requirement.

Floor:
2×10 floor joists @16" oc. wood bridging, 3/4 OSB T&G board, glued and nailed to joists.

Upper Floor Ceilings:
2×6 joists @16" oc, fiberglass insulation Blown/Batt (R-30*), wood strapping and 1/2" drywall, typical finish with spray/texture finish.
*R-30 on sloped area of shed roof.

Roof:
2×8/2×10 (per code) rafters/2×10 ridge, 5/8" OSB sheathing, water barrier on 1st 3' of roof and valleys, asphalt roof shingles (Slate color IKO Cambridge, Architectural/builders selection), perforated vinyl soffit and continuous ridge vent for ventilation (or comparable).

Exterior Walls:
7/16 siding sheathing on walls, vapor barrier and vinyl siding. Corners to be vinyl, soffit and gable trim to be wrapped.

Windows:
Double-hung vinyl-clad exterior insulated windows with screens and grills (Malta or equal).
Shutters optional.

Doors:
1-3' 2 light in front of home, insulated metal with hardwood/metal sill.
1-2'8" 9 light on side entrance, insulated metal with hardwood/metal sill.
1-2'8" metal at walkout entry in basement (if applicable), or metal bulkhead unit (actual style determined by contractor per site).
Interior Doors: 6 Panel Masonite.

Finish Work:

Interior door and window trim (picture frame) to be 2.5" colonial with 3.5" baseboard, finished with Antique White paint. Walls to be finished with a primer coat and a finish coat of Dover White paint (Sherwin Williams or equal).

Shelving and closets to be Closet Maid.

Contractor to provide plate glass mirrors over bath vanities.

Flooring:

Kitchen and bath areas where vinyl is to be applied will be pre-finished with 1/4" underlayment, sur-nailed to the existing sub-floor. Upper floor stairs to be pre-finished with 3/4" plywood treads/risers, glued and screwed to stringers. Railings, newel post, and spindles to be beech or equal with a painted finish (if applicable).

Lower level stairs to be finished with 2×10 treads and 2×4 skirt (safety) railings or drywall with one 1" milled hand rail.

Kitchen:

Kitchen cabinets are to be raised panel wood style with pre-formed Formica counter tops (per selections supplied). Soffits available upon request. No charge during framing stage.

Plumbing:

All necessary piping, venting, etc., for kitchens/baths indicated on plans. Jacuzzis/wetsinks, etc., extra. Copper water piping/PVC/ABS drainage piping or PEX Systme (builder's choice), Delta faucets or equal.

Baths:

Full baths to have one drop in sink, toilet, and a fiberglass tub/shower unit (bone typical). (Pedestal sink is optional but must be chosen prior to rough-in.)

Half bath to have one drop-in sink and toilet (typical).

All baths to have exhaust fan units.

Kitchen:

Hookup for dishwasher, double bowl SS sink with spray nozzle.

Heating System:
Weil-Mclain (or equal) FHW oil, power vented with domestic hot water per specs.
All plumbing, heating, and electrical work to be to code and performed by licensed installers where applicable.

Electrical:
200 amp overhead service.
Switched outlet in living room/bedrooms.
2 cable jacks.
2 telephone jacks.
All necessary wiring per code.

Allowances:
Flooring allowance: Vinyl and carpet allowance varies per house depending on square footage.
Typical allowance $18 per square yard calculated on square footage of home. (Sq. ftg. × 1.05% × allowance)
Lighting: $450 per home or supplied by builder.
Appliance allowance: Stove-dishwasher-range hood $700 or supplied by builder (Sears/Kenmore). Other appliances available at builder's cost (installation extra).
Well allowance $3,500.
Cabinet/vanity/countertop allowance $4,500 including installation.

Decks:
10×12 open deck with stairs and railings.
All decks to be built from pressure-treated wood. No finish required.
There will be a poured concrete step at base of stairs and poured concrete supports (sona tubs) where 4×4s meet ground. Built per site conditions.
Front steps to be pressure-treated wood or precast (builder's discretion).
Typical overhead garage doors if applicable (insulated rough sawn style).

Landscaping:
An allowance of $2,500 will be set up out of the contract for any imported loam, spreading, raking, and seeding. This allowance, which is included in the price of the home, will be held/disbursed by the bank to the customer/customer's landscaper upon completion of lawn. The allowance will be builder's only responsibility towards finished lawns. If customer desires, extensive landscaping and additional allowance can be built in in advance by request only.

Driveway is to be gravel with sides brought back to natural. Due to the difficulties in determining a cost to pave prior to construction any request for a paved drive cost will be an allowance only.

Additional Notes:

Two exterior faucets and two exterior electrical outlets are to be included, locations per site conditions.

Typical washer and dryer hookup in basement unless otherwise noted.

All groundwork (locating home on site, clearing, sloping, drainage areas, retaining walls, landscaping, etc.) is to be performed at builder's discretion.

Leachbed is to be installed by licensed installer per plans and specs (varies per site).

The above-mentioned specifications are not meant to include all materials in the home but simply a summary of comparable features. Also, the contractor must take into consideration applicable codes and regulations as well as typical construction practices for the area when ordering and reserves the right to make substitutions accordingly.

Any changes during construction must be approved in writing by builder prior to execution. Options are available to standard specifications but must be requested in writing from customer prior to construction. No verbal changes will be made. No blasting or ledge removal included.

Specification details available upon request.

If you need forms or contracts or just want to get some information from someone who isn't part of your deal, contact the National Association of Real Estate Agents at www.real estate agent.com. They have copies of contracts and forms that you can use free of charge. When you go to its Web site, you will find many options for forms, contracts, as well as listings for real estate agents and other people who can help you both locally and nationally.

Prefab Is Now Ab-Fab

Prefab is short for prefabricated, which means the house is built before it gets to the lot. Most homes, of course, are built on the spot. This on-the-spot building is part of what makes home construction expensive—a lot of people are involved, weather is a factor, and, when those two factors are combined a third problem arises: The process can be unpredictable and therefore time-consuming.

With prefabrication, the pieces of a home are built in a factory, so weather isn't a problem and there are fewer unpredictable elements. This can keep the price of the home down.

Unfortunately, however, prefab homes were first created in the early twentieth century (Sears, Roebuck actually sold them in their catalog), and they were considered cheap and tacky, especially when compared to other homes that were being built at the time, such as ornate Victorians and impressive Edwardians. Then, over the years, prefab became synonymous with mobile homes, which were small and stood grouped together in trailer parks—neighborhoods with bad reputations. Other prefab structures were just a notch above mobile homes: usually small houses made with cheap materials and sitting next to each other on small lots with little around them to increase their curb appeal or financial value.

The reason for this reputation was deserved, and it was born from a practical constraint: Prefab homes could only be as big as the packing containers they could be shipped in. A mobile home, for example, could only be the size of something that could actually be mobile. So, mobile homes are typically twelve to fifteen feet wide (or, in the case of doublewides, thirty feet), and while you own the home, you rent the land. Mobile homes are generally not well built, which is why, unfortunately, it is so common to see them fall apart during storms, high winds, or other natural, if intense, weather phenomena.

Nevertheless, throughout the twentieth century, numerous eminent architects, such as Corbusier, Wright, and Gropius, worked to improve the prefab house, because, to them, the concept seemed to be the way to create inexpensive homes that could potentially be modern and environmentally sound.

In the early twenty-first century, however, there has been a sort of prefab revolution. Architects have begun to see prefab housing as a cost-effective way to bring their designs to life.

The average site-built home costs $80 to $120 or more per square foot, while the average manufactured home costs $60 to $75. Typically, a prefab home can be built within three to six days and delivered in two to four months, about a third of the time it takes to produce a site-built home. Manufactured homes are turnkey, or ready for occupancy, the moment the owner walks through the door.

In fact, prefabs can look very handcrafted. While there are some limits (materials must endure those long truck rides), they can be styled as anything from colonial to Mediterranean, with brick or stone finishes added on with little fuss. Mobile homes do not appreciate the way stick-built homes do, although it is possible that modern prefabricated homes will increase in value in much the same way traditional houses do.

Builders and Architects

Few people want to build their own home with an actual hammer. And, we're pretty sure that if you do want to literally build your own home, then you're probably going to read a different book. So, we're going to assume that while you may want to build your own home, you also probably want someone else to do the actual building and, most likely, to find someone else to do the designing.

Having a home built exactly to your specifications is an expensive proposition, or, more to the point, generally more expensive than buying a home that has already been built. But, of course, to every rule there is an exception so if you have in mind that building your own home is what would make you happy, here are some things to understand before you do more research. (And we mean that: This is too big of an investment. It requires a lot of research, not just one chapter of a book.)

First, you can look into buying into a new home being built in a subdivision. These neighborhoods usually have options that allow you to choose between various models and styles of housing. So, while you aren't exactly designing the home from a light bulb idea in your head, you will have some say on the style (cape or contemporary?) of the home as well as its size. Plus, you can get specific in most cases on your particular needs, such as choosing to have an extra bathroom or adding a home office.

With this type of home, the developer usually offers a home warranty, which guarantees the work for a certain amount of time. Ten years is standard, but some developers will only offer one-year contracts. This kind of guarantee, which can cover items such as furnaces, the electrical system, and plumbing, helps to justify the higher price of a new home. Older homes will never come with this guarantee (or rarely do, unless the seller throws that in as an added bonus) and so you could move into a home and, the very next day, have to spend money for an unexpected expense, such as a broken heater or busted air conditioning system.

Here is a sample warranty:

The Builder/Seller, Raskin/Hawthorne Builders, Ltd., hereby limits warranties on the house and improvements on _____ _____ as follows and no other warranties, express or implied, or of merchantability or habitability are given except for statutory warranties of title made under the deed of conveyance:

1. INSPECTION AND REPAIR: Buyer acknowledges it has made a final visual inspection of the premises and the materials appear to be of good and satisfactory quality and the services and labor performed in a workmanlike manner. Buyer shall have fifteen (15) days from the date of transfer of title in which to compile a list discovered after moving into the premises. Buyer shall immediately thereafter notify Seller, and Seller shall repair or replace such items when and as may be reasonably practical.

2. MECHANICAL: Seller warrants the installation and materials of the mechanical devices, i.e., electrical wiring and fixture, plumbing and heating systems, for a period of one (1) year from the date of transfer of title. Faucet washers have no warranties.

3. STRUCTURE: The structure is defined as the poured concrete and framing materials contained in the house. Structural labor and materials are warranted by the Seller for three (3) years from the date

of transfer of title. Some settlement of base should be anticipated and hairline cracks in floors and walls, which do not undermine the structure, will not be repaired by the Seller.

4. SEPTIC AND LEACH: Seller warrants the septic system and leach field for two (2) years from the date of transfer of title, provided Buyer adequately maintains the septic system and has the septic tank pumped clean once a year.

5. WELLS: Seller warrants drinking water clear of bacteria with sufficient quantities for residential use for a period of one (1) year. However, Seller shall not be responsible for iron or magnesium buildups nor shall Seller be responsible for radon in the water.

6. BASEMENT: Seller has installed underground exterior perimeter drains to prevent accumulation of ground water around the basement floor and walls, but dampness and minor condensation cannot be prevented. Seller warrants for one (1) year against water in the basement, except for normal dampness and minor condensation. A dehumidifier is recommended to alleviate such buildup. In no event will Seller be liable for any damage caused by nearby blasting, earthquake, developing springs or substantial earth movement or damage caused by man-made or natural causes. Seller shall not be responsible for radon in the basement area.

7. APPLIANCES: Appliances installed by Seller have manufacturers' warranties and therefore Seller extends no warranties. Buyer shall deal directly with the respective manufacturers for repair or replacement according to the manufacturers' warranties.

8. CHIMNEY: Any chimneys installed by the Buyer or his/her agent carry no warranty by the Seller nor will Seller warrant against any damage caused by the faulty installation thereof. Seller installed chimneys shall carry a one (1) year warranty against defects in material and workmanship.

9. DRIVEWAY: Washouts of gravel driveways can occur as a result of inordinate rainfall or excessive watering. Any major washouts as

a result of inordinate earth settlement within six (6) months of the date of transfer of title shall be repaired by the Seller. Moderate top erosion is not warranted by Seller. Seller recommends blacktop at a future date when normal settlement has ended.

10. LANDSCAPING: Seller has installed a loam cover above ground base with sufficient grass seed to create a suitable lawn, but Seller does not guarantee against drought or washouts due to inordinate rainfall. Some minor earth settlement should be anticipated around the house foundation, and plantings should not be installed until sufficient time for settlement has elapsed.

11. SIDING: All siding is warranted for a period of one (1) year against defective materials and workmanship. Wood siding of any type is not warranted against shrinkage, bleaching, cracking, knots falling out, etc., since these are inherent characteristics of wood siding.

12. PAINTING: Because of shrinkage Seller applies only sufficient paint or stain to the exterior of the house to adequately cover. It is suggested that the Buyer repaint or restain the exterior of the house within one (1) year of occupancy to avoid deterioration of siding. No painting will be repaired unless it is specifically noted at the time of the preclosing inspection. Seller shall not be liable for marks or damage caused as a result of the Buyer moving into the premises.

13. MILLWORK: Millwork carries no warranties by the Seller including cracks or warpage. Where the Buyer intends to heat primarily or secondarily by wood stove it is recommended that a humidifier be installed in the winter to prevent inordinate cracks or warping of finish work.

14. ROOF: The roof is warranted for a period of three (3) years against leaks provided that Buyer does not install rooftop television antenna or other devices on the roof. Seller does not warrant against leaks due to ice buildup or backup due to severe winter weather.

15. FLOORING: The flooring underlayment has been surenailed, but Seller does not warrant against squeaks due to friction and

will not under any circumstances be responsible for removal or replacement of flooring.

16. WARRANTY LIMITED TO BUYER: The only warranties extended to the Buyer are those contained herein. Such warranties are extended to the Buyer only and are not assignable to any subsequent Buyer.

17. MATERIALS GENERALLY: The Seller has used material equal to or above State Code Specifications throughout the entire premises. The insulation does not contain urea-formaldehyde. However, some building materials contain urea-formaldehyde resin of which the Seller may be unaware. For some people urea-formaldehyde may cause health problems such as irritation of the eyes, nose, and throat; coughing, headaches, shortness of breath or chest stomach pains. Children under two (2) years of age, elderly persons with breathing problems, or persons with allergies may have more serious difficulties. If you have a question about problems you may have with urea-formaldehyde, consult a doctor.

The Buyer has read the warranties contained herein, understands them, and agrees to the conditions set forth.

IN WITNESS WHEREOF this_____ day of_____, XXXX.

_____   _____

Witness By: Company President

_____   _____

Witness Buyer

_____   _____

Witness Buyer

The other issue with homes built to order is that you're never quite sure when you're going to get to move in. While builders and developers will often give you a projected move-in date, there is no guarantee that the house will be done (or done as much as you would like it to be) according to schedule.

Whether you hire an architect or builder, you will need to have a list of everything you want in a home. You should bring this list with you and then refine it with the professionals you are interviewing. The list of attributes you want for the house will help the builder or architect figure out how much the house will cost as well as how long it will take to build.

Of course, you also need to figure out where you are going to build this home, and that means learning more about land and what houses need to be safe. For example, you need to make sure that your lot doesn't flood.

Before you meet with builders, you need to know the type of lot you want, the style of house you'd like, and some of its features and amenities.

It is most likely that the builders you meet with will have very different responses and ideas about your basic plans. Listen to them carefully and use both your head and your gut in deciding which builder would do the best work and work best for you. Don't feel funny about going back to each builder and explaining what you heard from the other people you've interviewed. This may help you get a better price and more honest information on what you can expect from the process.

You'll want to make sure that the builder doesn't use the phrase "subject to price variation" too often or that he doesn't write "or equal" too often, because this is a way they give themselves the option of not giving you what you asked for or not charging you what they promised. Also, check the price for "site work," which will have to be included, but shouldn't cost more than 10 percent of the total price. Because it's difficult to ascertain what this will add up to, you want to make sure this amount doesn't become infinite.

Now, you will have to go through the paperwork, just as someone who is buying an already-built home has to. The builder will most likely have a contract she works with, but you should bring that to a real estate attorney and make adjustments to make sure it's more even-handed. Some of the basic points of information you are looking for include:

- A start date for construction
- A construction end date

- A penalty clause for each day the home isn't finished after it is supposed to be
- A closing date (for the deal)
- A provision about your earnest money
- A contingency clause about financing

Like people who are buying already-built homes, you will need to create a list of things you want in your home, but you will have to add some specifics that are already given in built homes. For example, you'll want to decide on foundation type, siding, roof style and material, and what type of heating and cooling system you will use. Do you want sky lights or your home to be environmentally forward thinking, such as using solar panels? Sometimes local governments will give you breaks on utility pricing if you build a home that is energy efficient.

Most builders have a collection of plans that they have used before, and they will present these plans to you for review. A builder may require that your total loan, both for the lot and the house, be approved before he will start the project.

Just like looking for a real estate agent or mortgage lender, the most important thing about a builder is that you are confident she will create the house you wanted as closely as possible to the price you wanted in the time frame you agree upon. You should look at the body of this person's work and see if it jibes with the type of home you want. If you are interested in building an ecologically sound house, then you'll want a builder who wants that type of home in her portfolio. Your builder should respect your desires, not try to talk you into creating the house that is easiest for her to build.

Just as your real estate agent gets a commission, your builder also has to make money from this job. Builders usually base their pay on the appraisal of a home, expecting to receive 20 percent of the value of the house. Therefore, if you are building a $300,000 home, you can expect to pay the builder $60,000 after expenses. In other words, you aren't giving the builder just $60,000. You are paying whatever it costs to build the house, plus $60,000 to the builder.

Most homes take six months to a year to build, and you should expect a year to be the more likely amount of time. Obviously, the smaller the home, the shorter the amount of time, but, once again, all homebuilding is subject to weather delays.

One of the most important things to double check about your builder is that she will do everything up to code. You can go to the building code office of the town in which she has already worked to be sure there have been no problems with her work. Ask to get references for work she has previously done, and talk to other owners to find out what their experiences were like. Was the work done on time? Was the builder easy to communicate with? Did the owner get what she wanted?

There are tons of home plan books available and these are really fun to look at, because they give specific information about the options you'll have as a home designer. For example, the plans will include square feet, as well as options to make a house bigger or smaller in ways that work for you, such as a home office or mother-in-law apartment. Who will help you build your home?

- **Contractor/general contractor**—This person, who can be licensed, but doesn't have to be (although the laws can be different in each state), directs the construction, including the builder. The builder can also be the contractor, as can you.
- **Builder**—Not surprisingly, this is the person, usually connected to a company, who does the actual building.
- **Architect**—The person who designs the house. This person has to be licensed and usually has studied a great deal. Her skill involves not only listening to your needs and desires, but also understanding how to translate your dream into a safe and workable reality. The architect (and the builder) know how to make sure your realized dream will be up to code, satisfying both your imagination and the government's regulations (as well as general safety truths).
- **Subcontractors**—These are specialists who work on specific systems of the house, such as the plumbing or the electric. A contractor might bring this person onto the team, and he should let you know when he plans to do that and who the subcontractor is, as well as what his responsibilities will be. Subcontractors are experts in their particular areas, and they can even cover areas that you wouldn't expect such as HVAC, framing, and drywall.

Throughout the building process, you will have two inspectors visit you, one from the bank (to see where the money is going) and one from the local code officer (to make sure the home is being built according to plan).

When you build a home, you won't be exactly sure about what your taxes will be at the very end of the job, so stay in touch with your appraiser and local building department to make sure you are aware of their criteria for appraising and taxation.

If you do build a home you must make sure to get a certificate of occupancy (CO) at your close. This permit, issued by your local building office, deems the property suitable for habitation. The seller must provide this certification, but you should check on its status toward the end of the process. The close will not happen unless you have this paperwork in hand.

Audrey's Story:
"Upgrades are a serious profit center for builders."

Audrey Marten, 62, Sarasota, Florida

I love "new" homes. When I was married, we built two houses, but at this point I had been divorced for about nine years and living in a lovely maintenance-free community where the residents were dying at an alarming rate. Nice enough, but time to move on. I felt it was time for a new home before the "Home." Plus, I knew it would be a good saleable investment in the future should I decide a change was due.

Years ago when you built a home, you bought a lot in the area of your choice, contacted a builder, and then sketched out a general floor plan. The builder would give you a price, and then you signed on the dotted line and your home was built. The only thing you were able to choose was your flooring (vinyl, slate, or carpeting). Kitchens were the same, as were baths. They had wood cabinets and Formica countertops. Basic tubs and toilets. Not so today.

The model home era has arrived, and with it comes more choices. You really end up having mind-boggling decisions to make. This time around, I chose a gated community nearby that had some beautiful models with floor plans that worked for me. I worked through the various extras, such as special countertops and molding, the builders offered, which of course exceeded the standard. So this $265,000 home (in 2001) cost approximately 10 to 15 percent more than that.

I knew that I should be prepared to spend more than I thought I would, because unless you are disciplined it is easy to "upgrade" from the standard.

Everyone should be aware that upgrades are a real and serious profit center for builders. They actually make more proportionately from upgrades than on the basic package they show you at first.

Upgrades can include 20" tile rather than 12", stainless appliances, crown molding, custom paint choices, better carpeting, adding a paved driveway, enlarging the patio or just putting a window in for more daylight where you think you would like to have one.

In fact, I've learned that buyers should be careful about what is included and what is not and what the cost is to make changes. You shouldn't hesitate to tell each sales center representative that you are shopping around and comparing prices. Builders want your business, and sometimes you can make a better deal by just telling them what you want and what you can spend. That is rule number one.

The other thing that's really important is to look closely at the community you want to build in. For example, in retrospect, I don't think I chose the best community available. For starters it had only one amenity—a heated pool. And, for example, although the area is a gated enclave, it is located 500 yards off a busy highway and there is nowhere to walk. In fact, as I am writing this, I have contacted the county to get a sidewalk put in that would reach to the nearest traffic light. I hope it happens in my tenure!

If I were to choose again, I would be sure that the community had a clubhouse and as many activity choices as are available. For example, golf course communities are great here in hurricane Florida and have a built-in resale advantage. A clubhouse with a fitness area and tennis facilities are great, too. It is a super way to meet and network with others. Most communities offer bridge or other special interest activities. Depending where you are in life, go for as much as you can afford. It's great to come home after a workday and visit the main dining room for a cocktail and dinner.

That's why I always suggest that when buyers are making a decision about a house, they should ask themselves, "Why would anyone want to live here?" Don't get entranced by the pretties in the model. Look at the surrounding area. Check out the builder and find out more about her reputation.

Also choose an experienced real estate agent who knows the communities and the builders. She will be a great resource for comparison shopping. The agents are courted by the developers and can also show you the resale homes as well. Finally, look at resales. You do not get a better deal in a new development because you came in unescorted. This is a popular misconception. And bottom line, isn't it a good idea to talk over your options, pros and cons about this very important decision with someone you trust? ❧

part 3

Worksheets
and Sample Reports

How Much Home Can You Afford?

Equation: Monthly rent × 200 = Home price

This amount includes tax savings, so it's not as if the numbers will work out the same each month, but it will mean that it won't put you further in debt or cause you problems.

Another way to figure how much house you can afford:

1. Your gross monthly income   _____

2. Multiply by one of these percentages:

   - Conservative: 25% (.25)
   - Semi-conservative: 28% (.28)
   - If you have some debt: 33% (.33)
   - If you have extensive debt: 36% (.36)   _____

3. Now, with that final number, subtract any of these numbers:

   - Credit card debt (total from all cards)
   - Car payment
   - School loan payments
   - Other loan payments   _____

   The number you have here is how much you have available for your monthly mortgage payment.

4. Multiply this number by 12.   _____

5. Divide this number by your proposed interest rate. *(Remember to convert it to a decimal first.)* _____

   This is the total amount you have available for your mortgage.

6. Add amount you have for down payment._____

   This is the total amount you can spend on a house.

Mortgage Calculator

Remember, the number you arrive at below is just the amount you will pay for the principal and interest on your loan. It is not the full PITI payment and doesn't include taxes or insurance.

To get the amount of your monthly payment, find the interest rate you will be paying and the length of your loan, then multiply the number in that row/column by the amount of your loan, and divide by 1,000.

So, for example, if your loan will be for $275,000 and your loan is for thirty years at an interest rate of 5.25 percent, you will find the corresponding number in the chart below, which is 5.53. Next, multiply 5.53 by $275,000, which gives you $1,520,750. Divide this number by 1,000, and you find that your monthly payment, not including taxes or insurance, will be $1,520.75.

Length of Loan

%	15 years	30 years	40 years
5	7.91	5.37	4.83
5.25	8.04	5.53	4.99
5.5	8.18	5.68	5.16
5.75	8.31	5.84	5.33
6.0	8.44	6.00	5.50
6.25	8.57	6.16	5.68
6.5	8.71	6.32	5.85
6.75	8.85	6.49	6.03
7.0	8.99	6.65	6.21
7.25	9.13	6.82	6.40
7.5	9.27	6.99	6.58
7.75	9.41	7.16	6.77
8	9.56	7.34	6.95
8.25	9.70	7.51	7.14
8.5	9.85	7.69	7.34
8.75	10.00	7.87	7.53
9	10.15	8.05	7.72
9.25	10.30	8.23	7.91
9.5	10.45	8.41	8.11
9.75	10.60	8.60	8.30
10	10.75	8.78	8.50

Mortgage terms are not only done in 1/4 percent variations. You can get loans in 1/8, 7/8, or other increments, such as 5-7/8. There are numerous mortgage calculators on the Web that allow you to just plug in your numbers to find your payment. But, like this calculator, the number will not include your taxes and insurance. However, those calculators also include percentage points not on this list as well as other term lengths, such as twenty years.

What Will Your Monthly Expenses Be?

This form, which you can photocopy to use for each house you look at, takes into account all expenses you will have for a particular property. Some of the costs not related to the house (such as credit card bills or pet expenses) can be copied on each form. But don't neglect to include them, because this way, if you're choosing between purchasing two properties or trying to decide if a specific home is right for you, you will be able to see what your entire monthly budget will be. This is more helpful than simply looking at your mortgage payment. Also, some expenses, such as commuting costs or utility bills, can greatly affect your monthly budget.

Another thing: If you have annual expenses, such as car insurance, break down the cost by twelve so that you can figure it into your budget. Don't worry if you don't pay the bill monthly; this is just a way to make sure you aren't left hanging when the bill comes due.

This form doesn't include money that's coming in to you, so, we left a space at the bottom to remind you of how much money you have to use each month. After you buy a house, it's possible that amount will change because of tax changes, but it's better not to rely on that. Instead, use the amount you are living on now. Do not include money that is unreliable or generally unexpected, such as gifts.

Potential Monthly Expenses

Item	Cost	Item	Cost
House payment		Credit card bills	
Electricity		Commuting costs	
Oil heat		Medical insurance	
Gas heat		Dental insurance	
Phone		Pet expenses	
Snow removal		Hobbies/habits	
Water and sewer		Alimony	
Food		Clothes	
Computer		401(k)	
Cable		Child support	
Car payment		Health club	
Gas for car		Vacation	
Car repairs		Personal Savings	
Child care		Food	
Entertainment		School loans	
Home maintenance		Lawn care	
Trash pickup		Other	
Other		Other	
Column subtotal	_____	Column subtotal	_____
**Monthly Income	_____		
Total expenses	_____		

Names and Contact Information for Everyone on Your Team

Real estate agent:

Mortgage lender:

Banker:

Credit agencies:

Questions to Ask about Each House

Here's some space for you to keep notes and observations that you want to keep track of yourself.

What to Bring to the Close

- ☐ Proof of insurance
- ☐ Cashier's check (you cannot use personal checks at a close)
- ☐ Earnest money deposits
- ☐ The legal description of the property, including lot, block and section numbers (not just the address)
- ☐ Copy of the deed
- ☐ The title with all defects, liens, and judgments handled and resolved

Estimate of Closing Costs

Fill in these numbers to the best of your ability—ask the people involved—to give yourself an estimate of what you will be spending. Your real estate agent will offer you a good faith estimate herself, so you can compare your numbers to hers.

Item	Amount
Escrow	
Document preparation	
Loan origination	
Legal	
Loan assumption	
Transfer tax	
Pest control	
Loan application	
Recording	
Points	
Trustees	
Notary	
Prorated taxes	
Interest	
Mortgage insurance	
Inspection	
Credit report	
Hazard insurance	
Title insurance	
Down payment	
Other	
Subtotal (A)	

Credits	
Credits	
Credits	
Total credits (B)	
Estimated total cash needed for closing: (A) minus (B)	
Total estimated closing costs:	

What I Want in a House

Need	Desire

Loan Application Need Checklist

- ☐ Home addresses for the last five years
- ☐ Child support agreements
- ☐ Social Security numbers
- ☐ Tax returns from the past two years
- ☐ Paycheck stubs
- ☐ Employee tax statements, i.e., W-2s, W-4s
- ☐ Bank account numbers, balances, addresses, and the names attached
- ☐ Credit card numbers, balances, and monthly statements for three months
- ☐ Employment history for past five years
- ☐ Divorce agreements
- ☐ Stock/bond information
- ☐ 401(k) information
- ☐ Life insurance amounts
- ☐ Other loan information, such as car
- ☐ Credit card history
- ☐ Checkbooks (to pay fees)
- ☐ Investment property statement

Should I Rent? Live at Home? Or Buy?

Give a rating, on a scale of 1 to 20, for each item you put down in each column. You can use negatives for the "cons" column. Then, add up each column and subtract the negatives from the positives. See which option comes up with the highest number of points.

Buy a house			
Pros	Rating	Cons	Rating
subtotal		subtotal	
		Total Points	

Rent an apartment			
Pros	Rating	Cons	Rating
subtotal		subtotal	
		Total Points	

Live at home			
Pros	Rating	Cons	Rating
subtotal		subtotal	
		Total Points	

All My Loans

You should shop around for loans, just as you shop around for your house. This sheet will help you keep track of each loan you discuss.

Name of loan	Lender	Term of loan	Down payment	Interest rate	Adjustable rates	Prepayment penalty?	Points?	Pros/cons

Step-by-Step Process List

Item	Scheduled Date	Actual Date
Offer made		
Offer feedback		
Earnest money deposited		
Inspection		
Contingencies handled		
Loan application made		
Loan sent to underwriting		
Loan approval received		
Commitment letter sent		
Loan locked in		
Loan approval		
Title work started		
Title work completed		
Appraisal ordered		
Appraisal completed		
Insurance completed		
Scheduled closing		

Sample Offer Letter

THIS WRITTEN OFFER MUST BE PRESENTED TO THE SELLER IN ITS ENTIRETY INCLUDING THE COVER LETTER AND THE ENCLOSED MLS LISTING SHEET.

This offer is presented on this day, _____, to the Owner of Record of the land and buildings located at _____ as further described in book _____ page _____ certificate #__ _____ at the Registry of Deeds with as agent for the Seller. I will pay therefore $_____, of which

(a) $_____ is paid herewith as a deposit to bind this Offer.

(b) $_____ is to be paid as an additional deposit upon the execution of the Purchase and Sale Agreement.

(c) $_____ is to be paid at the time of delivery of the Deed in cash, or by certified, cashier's, treasurer's, or bank check(s).

(d) $_____ Total Purchase Price

Time for Performance of Offer

This offer is good until 6 P.M. on _____, at or before which time a copy hereof shall be signed by you, the Seller, signifying acceptance of this Offer, and returned to Buyer forthwith, otherwise this Offer shall be considered as rejected and the money deposited herewith shall be returned to Buyer forthwith.

Purchase and Sale Agreement

The parties hereto shall, on or before 6 P.M. on _____, execute a mutually agreeable Purchase and Sale Agreement to be drafted by the Seller's Representative (i.e., Attorney or Real Estate Broker) and to be presented to the Buyer for review and approval. The Buyer shall have at least five business days to review the Purchase and Sale Agreement prior to signing. If the terms and conditions are satisfactory to the Buyer, the Purchase and Sale shall be executed by the parties, and shall be the agreement between the parties hereto.

Conveyance of Deed

A good and sufficient Deed, conveying a good and clear record and marketable title shall be delivered at 12:00 noon on _____, at the Registry of Deeds, unless some other time and place are mutually agreed upon in writing.

Escrow

It is understood that all deposits and moneys will be held in an interest-bearing escrow account opened for this transaction, with all deposits and moneys not to be removed by any party until closing, rejection, or termination of this written agreement between the Buyer and Seller. Should the Seller and Buyer not enter into a satisfactory Purchase and Sale Agreement, all escrow funds will be returned to the Buyer, forthwith. All of the interest accrued will be paid to the Buyer at closing.

Mortgage Contingency

In order to help finance the acquisition of the property, the Buyer intends to apply for a conventional or other institutional loan of $_____, payable in no less than thirty years at an interest rate not to exceed the prevailing rate, acceptable to the Buyer. If despite the Buyer's diligent efforts, a written commitment for such a loan cannot be obtained for this property on or before _____, the Buyer shall have the option of revoking the Buyer's Offer by written notice to the Seller and/or the Seller's Broker, prior to the expiration of such time, whereupon all deposits made by the Buyer to you shall be forthwith refunded and this Offer shall become null and void without further recourse to the Buyer. The Buyer must submit a complete mortgage loan application conforming to the foregoing provisions within one week after signing the Purchase and Sale Agreement. Diligent efforts shall be satisfied so long as the Buyer applies to only one mortgage lender. This offer to purchase is made subject to the property being appraised by the Buyer's lender for at least the purchase price.

Home Inspection Contingency

The Buyer may at the Buyer's expense and within ten days after the Offer to Purchase has been signed by the Buyer and Seller, have the property inspected by persons engaged in the business of conducting home inspections. If it is the opinion of such inspectors that the property contains defects including: structural, mechanical, toxic or hazardous chemicals, radon gas, cesspool or septic defects, or other defects, then the Buyer shall have the option of revoking the Offer by written notice to the Seller and/or the Seller's Broker, prior to the expiration of such time, whereupon all deposits made by the Buyer to you shall be forthwith refunded, and this Offer shall become null and void and without further recourse to the Buyer.

Pest Inspection Contingency

The Buyer may, at the Buyer's own expense and within ten days after the Offer to Purchase has been signed by the Buyer and Seller, have the property inspected by a person engaged in the business of pest inspection or control. If it is of the opinion of such inspector that the property has been infested or damaged by termites or other pests, then the Buyer may terminate this agreement by written notice to the Seller and/or the Seller's Broker, prior to the expiration of such time, whereupon all deposits made by the Buyer to you shall be forthwith refunded, and this agreement shall become null and void and without further recourse to the Buyer unless the Seller agrees in writing to either treat the property to eliminate such infestation and repair all damage caused thereby to the Buyer's satisfaction or allow the Buyer credit against the purchase price sufficient to pay the reasonable cost of any such work not completed prior to the delivery of the Deed.

Title V and Flow Test (Private Sewer Systems Only)

If the premises contains a private sewer system, the Seller shall have the system inspected by a licensed Title V inspector satisfactory to the Seller and the city in which the property is located, for the purpose of verifying Title V compliance and proper operation determined by a Flow Test. This inspection will be at the Seller's sole cost with a copy of the written Title V and Flow Test report furnished to the Buyer. Subsequent to the inspection, all landscaping and work will be restored to its original condition. If the system does not pass Title V, a Flow Test, and operate in accordance with all applicable federal, state, and city codes, rules, and regulations, the Seller shall correct the system to proper operation and comply with applicable codes, rules, and regulations or this transaction will become null and void and all deposits made by the Buyer to you shall be forthwith refunded, and this Offer shall become null and void and without further recourse to the Buyer.

Manuals and Warranties

The Seller agrees to deliver to the Buyer at the time of delivery of Deed any copies of directions, manuals, and warranties in the Seller's possession for all appliances, fixtures, equipment, and materials including but not limited to the garbage disposal, dishwasher, stove, furnace, water heater, garage door openers, and building materials.

Plot Plan and Deed

Seller shall provide Buyer with a copy of the certified plot plan and deed for the property for Buyer's review/approval.

Building Permits

Seller shall provide Buyer with copies of building permits for any renovations or repairs to the home/property during the time the Seller owned the property, if permits were required by building code or city ordinance. A few examples of work that may require building permits are deck and/or porch renovation or construction, structural renovations or repairs to the dwelling, electrical or plumbing work, installation of a wood stove or fireplace, and installation of a swimming pool.

Home Warranty

The Seller hereby agrees to pay $_____ for a 1 Year HMS Preferred Plus Home Warranty, which will cover the oven/range, built-in microwave, built-in dishwasher, washer/dryer, built-in trash compactor, refrigerator, doorbell chime, hot water heater, garbage disposal, central vacuum, electrical system, paddle fans, garage door opener, faucets, plumbing system, air conditioning, heating system, and the water softener for the Buyer.

Additional Contingencies (if any):

Inspection Checklist

You might not understand some of these words and terms, so ask the inspector what each term means and go around with him to see what he notices. Ask him to show you exactly what he's looking at and what's right and what's wrong about each detail.

The Roof

- Is the roof straight and level?
- Is the roof sagging between the rafters or trusses?
- Are there any signs of deterioration of asphalt shingles, such as curling, wasping, broken edges, rounded corners, or key holes (slits) becoming wider than normal?
- Anything loose at the chimney, roof-to-wall connection, or elsewhere?
- Does the wooden roof deck appear rotten or delaminated under the last row of shingles?
- Are there any roof vents visible?

The Chimney

- Is the masonry cap cracked or broken?
- Are any bricks flaking or missing? Mortar missing?
- Is the chimney leaning?

Siding

- Is it made of wood, aluminum, or plastic?
- Are there any loose or missing sections?
- If it's wood, are there any paint problems? Any visible rot?

The Gutters

- Do gutters slope down toward downspouts?
- Is there any rust or peeling paint?
- Are there apparent leaks or loose/sagging sections?
- Are the downspouts extended away from the foundation?

The Outside Walls

- Is any mortar missing?
- Are the bricks flaking or cracking?
- Is there any loose, missing or rotten siding or deteriorated paint?
- Does the siding appear new? Does it hide the foundation wall?
- Are the exterior walls bowed, bulged, or leaning?

The Windows and Doors

- Are there any problems with paint or caulking or any rotted wood components?
- Are the windows new or older? Are they the original windows? How old are they?

The Porches and Decks

- Is the masonry cracking or flaking?
- Are there problems with paint, rotted wood, or wood-earth contact?
- Is there any settlement or separation from the house?
- Inspect the underside, if accessible.

The Foundation

- Are there any cracks? Is the masonry flaking or damaged?
- Are there any water markings or residue from water leaks?
- Any bowing, bulging, or other irregularities?
- Any soft mortar?

The Lot

- Does the grade slope away from the house?
- Any settled/low areas next to the foundation, or cracked walks/driveway?
- Is the property lower than the street or neighboring properties?

The Basement

- Is there any evidence of water penetration (stains, mildew/odors, loose tiles, etc.)?

The Interior Floors

- Are there deteriorated coverings or cracked ceramics?
- Any water staining or other damage?
- Any sloping or sagging?

The Interior Walls

- Randomly sample to check that the windows and doors work.
- Are the walls straight vertically and horizontally?
- Is there any cracked or loose plaster?
- Any stains, physical damage, or evidence of previous repair?
- Any drywall seams or nails showing?

The Interior Ceilings

- Are there any cracks in the plaster or is the plaster loose or sagging?
- Are there stains, mechanical damage, or evidence of previous repair?
- Any seams or nails showing?

The Bathrooms and Kitchen

- Are there any cracks in the fixtures?
- What is the condition of the tiles and caulking in the tub/shower area?
- Are the faucets working? Do they leak? Is there sufficient water pressure?
- Is there staining or rot under the countertops?
- Randomly sample the operation of the cabinet doors and drawers.

The Electrical

- Note the type, style, and age of heating and cooling systems. When were they last inspected or serviced?
- Note the type of water supply piping and drains. Is there any visible rust or corrosion?
- Note the size and age of electrical service. Are the outlets grounded? Is visible wiring in good condition?
- Have there been any upgrades?

Mortgage Tables

Interest Rate: 6.00%

Amount Borrowed	Length of Loan (in Years)					
	5	10	15	20	25	30
$50,000	$966.64	$555.10	$421.93	$358.22	$322.15	$299.78
$60,000	$1,159.97	$666.12	$506.31	$429.86	$386.58	$359.73
$70,000	$1,353.30	$777.14	$590.70	$501.50	$451.01	$419.69
$80,000	$1,546.62	$888.16	$675.09	$573.14	$515.44	$479.64
$90,000	$1,739.95	$999.18	$759.47	$644.79	$579.87	$539.60
$100,000	$1,933.28	$1,110.21	$843.86	$716.43	$644.30	$599.55
$110,000	$2,126.61	$1,221.23	$928.24	$788.07	$708.73	$659.51
$120,000	$2,319.94	$1,332.25	$1,012.63	$859.72	$773.16	$719.46
$130,000	$2,513.26	$1,443.27	$1,097.01	$931.36	$837.59	$779.42
$140,000	$2,706.59	$1,554.29	$1,181.40	$1,003.00	$902.02	$839.37
$150,000	$2,899.92	$1,665.31	$1,265.79	$1,074.65	$966.45	$899.33
$160,000	$3,093.25	$1,776.33	$1,350.17	$1,146.29	$1,030.88	$959.28
$170,000	$3,286.58	$1,887.35	$1,434.56	$1,217.93	$1,095.31	$1,019.24
$180,000	$3,479.90	$1,998.37	$1,518.94	$1,289.58	$1,159.74	$1,079.19
$190,000	$3,673.23	$2,109.39	$1,603.33	$1,361.22	$1,224.17	$1,139.15
$200,000	$3,866.56	$2,220.41	$1,687.71	$1,432.86	$1,288.60	$1,199.10
$210,000	$4,059.89	$2,331.43	$1,772.10	$1,504.51	$1,353.03	$1,259.06
$220,000	$4,253.22	$2,442.45	$1,856.49	$1,576.15	$1,417.46	$1,319.01
$230,000	$4,446.54	$2,553.47	$1,940.87	$1,647.79	$1,481.89	$1,378.97
$240,000	$4,639.87	$2,664.49	$2,025.26	$1,719.43	$1,546.32	$1,438.92
$250,000	$4,833.20	$2,775.51	$2,109.64	$1,791.08	$1,610.75	$1,498.88
$260,000	$5,026.53	$2,886.53	$2,194.03	$1,862.72	$1,675.18	$1,558.83
$270,000	$5,219.86	$2,997.55	$2,278.41	$1,934.36	$1,739.61	$1,618.79
$280,000	$5,413.18	$3,108.57	$2,362.80	$2,006.01	$1,804.04	$1,678.74
$290,000	$5,606.51	$3,219.59	$2,447.18	$2,077.65	$1,868.47	$1,738.70
$300,000	$5,799.84	$3,330.62	$2,531.57	$2,149.29	$1,932.90	$1,798.65
$310,000	$5,993.17	$3,441.64	$2,615.96	$2,220.94	$1,997.33	$1,858.61

Interest Rate: 6.50%

Amount Borrowed	Length of Loan (in Years)					
	5	10	15	20	25	30
$50,000	$978.31	$567.74	$435.55	$372.79	$337.60	$316.03
$60,000	$1,173.97	$681.29	$522.66	$447.34	$405.12	$379.24
$70,000	$1,369.63	$794.84	$609.78	$521.90	$472.65	$442.45
$80,000	$1,565.29	$908.38	$696.89	$596.46	$540.17	$505.65
$90,000	$1,760.95	$1,021.93	$784.00	$671.02	$607.69	$568.86
$100,000	$1,956.61	$1,135.48	$871.11	$745.57	$675.21	$632.07
$110,000	$2,152.28	$1,249.03	$958.22	$820.13	$742.73	$695.27
$120,000	$2,347.94	$1,362.58	$1,045.33	$894.69	$810.25	$758.48
$130,000	$2,543.60	$1,476.12	$1,132.44	$969.25	$877.77	$821.69
$140,000	$2,739.26	$1,589.67	$1,219.55	$1,043.80	$945.29	$884.90
$150,000	$2,934.92	$1,703.22	$1,306.66	$1,118.36	$1,012.81	$948.10
$160,000	$3,130.58	$1,816.77	$1,393.77	$1,192.92	$1,080.33	$1,011.31
$170,000	$3,326.25	$1,930.32	$1,480.88	$1,267.47	$1,147.85	$1,074.52
$180,000	$3,521.91	$2,043.86	$1,567.99	$1,342.03	$1,215.37	$1,137.72
$190,000	$3,717.57	$2,157.41	$1,655.10	$1,416.59	$1,282.89	$1,200.93
$200,000	$3,913.23	$2,270.96	$1,742.21	$1,491.15	$1,350.41	$1,264.14
$210,000	$4,108.89	$2,384.51	$1,829.33	$1,565.70	$1,417.94	$1,327.34
$220,000	$4,304.55	$2,498.06	$1,916.44	$1,640.26	$1,485.46	$1,390.55
$230,000	$4,500.21	$2,611.60	$2,003.55	$1,714.82	$1,552.98	$1,453.76
$240,000	$4,695.88	$2,725.15	$2,090.66	$1,789.38	$1,620.50	$1,516.96
$250,000	$4,891.54	$2,838.70	$2,177.77	$1,863.93	$1,688.02	$1,580.17
$260,000	$5,087.20	$2,952.25	$2,264.88	$1,938.49	$1,755.54	$1,643.38
$270,000	$5,282.86	$3,065.80	$2,351.99	$2,013.05	$1,823.06	$1,706.58
$280,000	$5,478.52	$3,179.34	$2,439.10	$2,087.60	$1,890.58	$1,769.79
$290,000	$5,674.18	$3,292.89	$2,526.21	$2,162.16	$1,958.10	$1,833.00
$300,000	$5,869.84	$3,406.44	$2,613.32	$2,236.72	$2,025.62	$1,896.20
$310,000	$6,065.51	$3,519.99	$2,700.43	$2,311.28	$2,093.14	$1,959.41

Interest Rate: 7.00%

Amount Borrowed	Length of Loan (in Years)					
	5	10	15	20	25	30
$50,000	$990.06	$580.54	$449.41	$387.65	$353.39	$332.65
$60,000	$1,188.07	$696.65	$539.30	$465.18	$424.07	$399.18
$70,000	$1,386.08	$812.76	$629.18	$542.71	$494.75	$465.71
$80,000	$1,584.10	$928.87	$719.06	$620.24	$565.42	$532.24
$90,000	$1,782.11	$1,044.98	$808.95	$697.77	$636.10	$598.77
$100,000	$1,980.12	$1,161.08	$898.83	$775.30	$706.78	$665.30
$110,000	$2,178.13	$1,277.19	$988.71	$852.83	$777.46	$731.83
$120,000	$2,376.14	$1,393.30	$1,078.59	$930.36	$848.14	$798.36
$130,000	$2,574.16	$1,509.41	$1,168.48	$1,007.89	$918.81	$864.89
$140,000	$2,772.17	$1,625.52	$1,258.36	$1,085.42	$989.49	$931.42
$150,000	$2,970.18	$1,741.63	$1,348.24	$1,162.95	$1,060.17	$997.95
$160,000	$3,168.19	$1,857.74	$1,438.13	$1,240.48	$1,130.85	$1,064.48
$170,000	$3,366.20	$1,973.84	$1,528.01	$1,318.01	$1,201.52	$1,131.01
$180,000	$3,564.22	$2,089.95	$1,617.89	$1,395.54	$1,272.20	$1,197.54
$190,000	$3,762.23	$2,206.06	$1,707.77	$1,473.07	$1,342.88	$1,264.07
$200,000	$3,960.24	$2,322.17	$1,797.66	$1,550.60	$1,413.56	$1,330.60
$210,000	$4,158.25	$2,438.28	$1,887.54	$1,628.13	$1,484.24	$1,397.14
$220,000	$4,356.26	$2,554.39	$1,977.42	$1,705.66	$1,554.91	$1,463.67
$230,000	$4,554.28	$2,670.50	$2,067.31	$1,783.19	$1,625.59	$1,530.20
$240,000	$4,752.29	$2,786.60	$2,157.19	$1,860.72	$1,696.27	$1,596.73
$250,000	$4,950.30	$2,902.71	$2,247.07	$1,938.25	$1,766.95	$1,663.26
$260,000	$5,148.31	$3,018.82	$2,336.95	$2,015.78	$1,837.63	$1,729.79
$270,000	$5,346.32	$3,134.93	$2,426.84	$2,093.31	$1,908.30	$1,796.32
$280,000	$5,544.34	$3,251.04	$2,516.72	$2,170.84	$1,978.98	$1,862.85
$290,000	$5,742.35	$3,367.15	$2,606.60	$2,248.37	$2,049.66	$1,929.38
$300,000	$5,940.36	$3,483.25	$2,696.48	$2,325.90	$2,120.34	$1,995.91
$310,000	$6,138.37	$3,599.36	$2,786.37	$2,403.43	$2,191.02	$2,062.44

Interest Rate: 7.50%

Amount Borrowed	Length of Loan (in Years)					
	5	10	15	20	25	30
$50,000	$1,001.90	$593.51	$463.51	$402.80	$369.50	$349.61
$60,000	$1,202.28	$712.21	$556.21	$483.36	$443.39	$419.53
$70,000	$1,402.66	$830.91	$648.91	$563.92	$517.29	$489.45
$80,000	$1,603.04	$949.61	$741.61	$644.47	$591.19	$559.37
$90,000	$1,803.42	$1,068.32	$834.31	$725.03	$665.09	$629.29
$100,000	$2,003.79	$1,187.02	$927.01	$805.59	$738.99	$699.21
$110,000	$2,204.17	$1,305.72	$1,019.71	$886.15	$812.89	$769.14
$120,000	$2,404.55	$1,424.42	$1,112.41	$966.71	$886.79	$839.06
$130,000	$2,604.93	$1,543.12	$1,205.12	$1,047.27	$960.69	$908.98
$140,000	$2,805.31	$1,661.82	$1,297.82	$1,127.83	$1,034.59	$978.90
$150,000	$3,005.69	$1,780.53	$1,390.52	$1,208.39	$1,108.49	$1,048.82
$160,000	$3,206.07	$1,899.23	$1,483.22	$1,288.95	$1,182.39	$1,118.74
$170,000	$3,406.45	$2,017.93	$1,575.92	$1,369.51	$1,256.29	$1,188.66
$180,000	$3,606.83	$2,136.63	$1,668.62	$1,450.07	$1,330.18	$1,258.59
$190,000	$3,807.21	$2,255.33	$1,761.32	$1,530.63	$1,404.08	$1,328.51
$200,000	$4,007.59	$2,374.04	$1,854.02	$1,611.19	$1,477.98	$1,398.43
$210,000	$4,207.97	$2,492.74	$1,946.73	$1,691.75	$1,551.88	$1,468.35
$220,000	$4,408.35	$2,611.44	$2,039.43	$1,772.31	$1,625.78	$1,538.27
$230,000	$4,608.73	$2,730.14	$2,132.13	$1,852.86	$1,699.68	$1,608.19
$240,000	$4,809.11	$2,848.84	$2,224.83	$1,933.42	$1,773.58	$1,678.11
$250,000	$5,009.49	$2,967.54	$2,317.53	$2,013.98	$1,847.48	$1,748.04
$260,000	$5,209.87	$3,086.25	$2,410.23	$2,094.54	$1,921.38	$1,817.96
$270,000	$5,410.25	$3,204.95	$2,502.93	$2,175.10	$1,995.28	$1,887.88
$280,000	$5,610.63	$3,323.65	$2,595.63	$2,255.66	$2,069.18	$1,957.80
$290,000	$5,811.01	$3,442.35	$2,688.34	$2,336.22	$2,143.07	$2,027.72
$300,000	$6,011.38	$3,561.05	$2,781.04	$2,416.78	$2,216.97	$2,097.64
$310,000	$6,211.76	$3,679.75	$2,873.74	$2,497.34	$2,290.87	$2,167.56

Interest Rate: 8.00%

Amount Borrowed	Length of Loan (in Years)					
	5	10	15	20	25	30
$50,000	$1,013.82	$606.64	$477.83	$418.22	$385.91	$366.88
$60,000	$1,216.58	$727.97	$573.39	$501.86	$463.09	$440.26
$70,000	$1,419.35	$849.29	$668.96	$585.51	$540.27	$513.64
$80,000	$1,622.11	$970.62	$764.52	$669.15	$617.45	$587.01
$90,000	$1,824.88	$1,091.95	$860.09	$752.80	$694.63	$660.39
$100,000	$2,027.64	$1,213.28	$955.65	$836.44	$771.82	$733.76
$110,000	$2,230.40	$1,334.60	$1,051.22	$920.08	$849.00	$807.14
$120,000	$2,433.17	$1,455.93	$1,146.78	$1,003.73	$926.18	$880.52
$130,000	$2,635.93	$1,577.26	$1,242.35	$1,087.37	$1,003.36	$953.89
$140,000	$2,838.70	$1,698.59	$1,337.91	$1,171.02	$1,080.54	$1,027.27
$150,000	$3,041.46	$1,819.91	$1,433.48	$1,254.66	$1,157.72	$1,100.65
$160,000	$3,244.22	$1,941.24	$1,529.04	$1,338.30	$1,234.91	$1,174.02
$170,000	$3,446.99	$2,062.57	$1,624.61	$1,421.95	$1,312.09	$1,247.40
$180,000	$3,649.75	$2,183.90	$1,720.17	$1,505.59	$1,389.27	$1,320.78
$190,000	$3,852.51	$2,305.22	$1,815.74	$1,589.24	$1,466.45	$1,394.15
$200,000	$4,055.28	$2,426.55	$1,911.30	$1,672.88	$1,543.63	$1,467.53
$210,000	$4,258.04	$2,547.88	$2,006.87	$1,756.52	$1,620.81	$1,540.91
$220,000	$4,460.81	$2,669.21	$2,102.43	$1,840.17	$1,698.00	$1,614.28
$230,000	$4,663.57	$2,790.53	$2,198.00	$1,923.81	$1,775.18	$1,687.66
$240,000	$4,866.33	$2,911.86	$2,293.57	$2,007.46	$1,852.36	$1,761.03
$250,000	$5,069.10	$3,033.19	$2,389.13	$2,091.10	$1,929.54	$1,834.41
$260,000	$5,271.86	$3,154.52	$2,484.70	$2,174.74	$2,006.72	$1,907.79
$270,000	$5,474.63	$3,275.85	$2,580.26	$2,258.39	$2,083.90	$1,981.16
$280,000	$5,677.39	$3,397.17	$2,675.83	$2,342.03	$2,161.09	$2,054.54
$290,000	$5,880.15	$3,518.50	$2,771.39	$2,425.68	$2,238.27	$2,127.92
$300,000	$6,082.92	$3,639.83	$2,866.96	$2,509.32	$2,315.45	$2,201.29
$310,000	$6,285.68	$3,761.16	$2,962.52	$2,592.96	$2,392.63	$2,274.67

Interest Rate: 8.50%

Amount Borrowed	Length of Loan (in Years)					
	5	10	15	20	25	30
$50,000	$1,025.83	$619.93	$492.37	$433.91	$402.61	$384.46
$60,000	$1,230.99	$743.91	$590.84	$520.69	$483.14	$461.35
$70,000	$1,436.16	$867.90	$689.32	$607.48	$563.66	$538.24
$80,000	$1,641.32	$991.89	$787.79	$694.26	$644.18	$615.13
$90,000	$1,846.49	$1,115.87	$886.27	$781.04	$724.70	$692.02
$100,000	$2,051.65	$1,239.86	$984.74	$867.82	$805.23	$768.91
$110,000	$2,256.82	$1,363.84	$1,083.21	$954.61	$885.75	$845.80
$120,000	$2,461.98	$1,487.83	$1,181.69	$1,041.39	$966.27	$922.70
$130,000	$2,667.15	$1,611.81	$1,280.16	$1,128.17	$1,046.80	$999.59
$140,000	$2,872.31	$1,735.80	$1,378.64	$1,214.95	$1,127.32	$1,076.48
$150,000	$3,077.48	$1,859.79	$1,477.11	$1,301.73	$1,207.84	$1,153.37
$160,000	$3,282.65	$1,983.77	$1,575.58	$1,388.52	$1,288.36	$1,230.26
$170,000	$3,487.81	$2,107.76	$1,674.06	$1,475.30	$1,368.89	$1,307.15
$180,000	$3,692.98	$2,231.74	$1,772.53	$1,562.08	$1,449.41	$1,384.04
$190,000	$3,898.14	$2,355.73	$1,871.01	$1,648.86	$1,529.93	$1,460.94
$200,000	$4,103.31	$2,479.71	$1,969.48	$1,735.65	$1,610.45	$1,537.83
$210,000	$4,308.47	$2,603.70	$2,067.95	$1,822.43	$1,690.98	$1,614.72
$220,000	$4,513.64	$2,727.69	$2,166.43	$1,909.21	$1,771.50	$1,691.61
$230,000	$4,718.80	$2,851.67	$2,264.90	$1,995.99	$1,852.02	$1,768.50
$240,000	$4,923.97	$2,975.66	$2,363.37	$2,082.78	$1,932.55	$1,845.39
$250,000	$5,129.13	$3,099.64	$2,461.85	$2,169.56	$2,013.07	$1,922.28
$260,000	$5,334.30	$3,223.63	$2,560.32	$2,256.34	$2,093.59	$1,999.18
$270,000	$5,539.46	$3,347.61	$2,658.80	$2,343.12	$2,174.11	$2,076.07
$280,000	$5,744.63	$3,471.60	$2,757.27	$2,429.91	$2,254.64	$2,152.96
$290,000	$5,949.79	$3,595.58	$2,855.74	$2,516.69	$2,335.16	$2,229.85
$300,000	$6,154.96	$3,719.57	$2,954.22	$2,603.47	$2,415.68	$2,306.74
$310,000	$6,360.12	$3,843.56	$3,052.69	$2,690.25	$2,496.20	$2,383.63

Interest Rate: 9.00%

Amount Borrowed	Length of Loan (in Years)					
	5	10	15	20	25	30
$50,000	$1,037.92	$633.38	$507.13	$449.86	$419.60	$402.31
$60,000	$1,245.50	$760.05	$608.56	$539.84	$503.52	$482.77
$70,000	$1,453.08	$886.73	$709.99	$629.81	$587.44	$563.24
$80,000	$1,660.67	$1,013.41	$811.41	$719.78	$671.36	$643.70
$90,000	$1,868.25	$1,140.08	$912.84	$809.75	$755.28	$724.16
$100,000	$2,075.84	$1,266.76	$1,014.27	$899.73	$839.20	$804.62
$110,000	$2,283.42	$1,393.43	$1,115.69	$989.70	$923.12	$885.08
$120,000	$2,491.00	$1,520.11	$1,217.12	$1,079.67	$1,007.04	$965.55
$130,000	$2,698.59	$1,646.79	$1,318.55	$1,169.64	$1,090.96	$1,046.01
$140,000	$2,906.17	$1,773.46	$1,419.97	$1,259.62	$1,174.87	$1,126.47
$150,000	$3,113.75	$1,900.14	$1,521.40	$1,349.59	$1,258.79	$1,206.93
$160,000	$3,321.34	$2,026.81	$1,622.83	$1,439.56	$1,342.71	$1,287.40
$170,000	$3,528.92	$2,153.49	$1,724.25	$1,529.53	$1,426.63	$1,367.86
$180,000	$3,736.50	$2,280.16	$1,825.68	$1,619.51	$1,510.55	$1,448.32
$190,000	$3,944.09	$2,406.84	$1,927.11	$1,709.48	$1,594.47	$1,528.78
$200,000	$4,151.67	$2,533.52	$2,028.53	$1,799.45	$1,678.39	$1,609.25
$210,000	$4,359.25	$2,660.19	$2,129.96	$1,889.42	$1,762.31	$1,689.71
$220,000	$4,566.84	$2,786.87	$2,231.39	$1,979.40	$1,846.23	$1,770.17
$230,000	$4,774.42	$2,913.54	$2,332.81	$2,069.37	$1,930.15	$1,850.63
$240,000	$4,982.01	$3,040.22	$2,434.24	$2,159.34	$2,014.07	$1,931.09
$250,000	$5,189.59	$3,166.89	$2,535.67	$2,249.31	$2,097.99	$2,011.56
$260,000	$5,397.17	$3,293.57	$2,637.09	$2,339.29	$2,181.91	$2,092.02
$270,000	$5,604.76	$3,420.25	$2,738.52	$2,429.26	$2,265.83	$2,172.48
$280,000	$5,812.34	$3,546.92	$2,839.95	$2,519.23	$2,349.75	$2,252.94
$290,000	$6,019.92	$3,673.60	$2,941.37	$2,609.21	$2,433.67	$2,333.41
$300,000	$6,227.51	$3,800.27	$3,042.80	$2,699.18	$2,517.59	$2,413.87
$310,000	$6,435.09	$3,926.95	$3,144.23	$2,789.15	$2,601.51	$2,494.33

Interest Rate: 9.50%

Amount Borrowed	Length of Loan (in Years)					
	5	10	15	20	25	30
$50,000	$1,050.09	$646.99	$522.11	$466.07	$436.85	$420.43
$60,000	$1,260.11	$776.39	$626.53	$559.28	$524.22	$504.51
$70,000	$1,470.13	$905.78	$730.96	$652.49	$611.59	$588.60
$80,000	$1,680.15	$1,035.18	$835.38	$745.70	$698.96	$672.68
$90,000	$1,890.17	$1,164.58	$939.80	$838.92	$786.33	$756.77
$100,000	$2,100.19	$1,293.98	$1,044.22	$932.13	$873.70	$840.85
$110,000	$2,310.20	$1,423.37	$1,148.65	$1,025.34	$961.07	$924.94
$120,000	$2,520.22	$1,552.77	$1,253.07	$1,118.56	$1,048.44	$1,009.03
$130,000	$2,730.24	$1,682.17	$1,357.49	$1,211.77	$1,135.81	$1,093.11
$140,000	$2,940.26	$1,811.57	$1,461.91	$1,304.98	$1,223.18	$1,177.20
$150,000	$3,150.28	$1,940.96	$1,566.34	$1,398.20	$1,310.54	$1,261.28
$160,000	$3,360.30	$2,070.36	$1,670.76	$1,491.41	$1,397.91	$1,345.37
$170,000	$3,570.32	$2,199.76	$1,775.18	$1,584.62	$1,485.28	$1,429.45
$180,000	$3,780.34	$2,329.16	$1,879.60	$1,677.84	$1,572.65	$1,513.54
$190,000	$3,990.35	$2,458.55	$1,984.03	$1,771.05	$1,660.02	$1,597.62
$200,000	$4,200.37	$2,587.95	$2,088.45	$1,864.26	$1,747.39	$1,681.71
$210,000	$4,410.39	$2,717.35	$2,192.87	$1,957.48	$1,834.76	$1,765.79
$220,000	$4,620.41	$2,846.75	$2,297.29	$2,050.69	$1,922.13	$1,849.88
$230,000	$4,830.43	$2,976.14	$2,401.72	$2,143.90	$2,009.50	$1,933.96
$240,000	$5,040.45	$3,105.54	$2,506.14	$2,237.11	$2,096.87	$2,018.05
$250,000	$5,250.47	$3,234.94	$2,610.56	$2,330.33	$2,184.24	$2,102.14
$260,000	$5,460.48	$3,364.34	$2,714.98	$2,423.54	$2,271.61	$2,186.22
$270,000	$5,670.50	$3,493.73	$2,819.41	$2,516.75	$2,358.98	$2,270.31
$280,000	$5,880.52	$3,623.13	$2,923.83	$2,609.97	$2,446.35	$2,354.39
$290,000	$6,090.54	$3,752.53	$3,028.25	$2,703.18	$2,533.72	$2,438.48
$300,000	$6,300.56	$3,881.93	$3,132.67	$2,796.39	$2,621.09	$2,522.56
$310,000	$6,510.58	$4,011.32	$3,237.10	$2,889.61	$2,708.46	$2,606.65

Interest Rate: 10.00%

Amount Borrowed	Length of Loan (in Years)					
	5	10	15	20	25	30
$50,000	$1,062.35	$660.75	$537.30	$482.51	$454.35	$438.79
$60,000	$1,274.82	$792.90	$644.76	$579.01	$545.22	$526.54
$70,000	$1,487.29	$925.06	$752.22	$675.52	$636.09	$614.30
$80,000	$1,699.76	$1,057.21	$859.68	$772.02	$726.96	$702.06
$90,000	$1,912.23	$1,189.36	$967.14	$868.52	$817.83	$789.81
$100,000	$2,124.70	$1,321.51	$1,074.61	$965.02	$908.70	$877.57
$110,000	$2,337.17	$1,453.66	$1,182.07	$1,061.52	$999.57	$965.33
$120,000	$2,549.65	$1,585.81	$1,289.53	$1,158.03	$1,090.44	$1,053.09
$130,000	$2,762.12	$1,717.96	$1,396.99	$1,254.53	$1,181.31	$1,140.84
$140,000	$2,974.59	$1,850.11	$1,504.45	$1,351.03	$1,272.18	$1,228.60
$150,000	$3,187.06	$1,982.26	$1,611.91	$1,447.53	$1,363.05	$1,316.36
$160,000	$3,399.53	$2,114.41	$1,719.37	$1,544.03	$1,453.92	$1,404.11
$170,000	$3,612.00	$2,246.56	$1,826.83	$1,640.54	$1,544.79	$1,491.87
$180,000	$3,824.47	$2,378.71	$1,934.29	$1,737.04	$1,635.66	$1,579.63
$190,000	$4,036.94	$2,510.86	$2,041.75	$1,833.54	$1,726.53	$1,667.39
$200,000	$4,249.41	$2,643.01	$2,149.21	$1,930.04	$1,817.40	$1,755.14
$210,000	$4,461.88	$2,775.17	$2,256.67	$2,026.55	$1,908.27	$1,842.90
$220,000	$4,674.35	$2,907.32	$2,364.13	$2,123.05	$1,999.14	$1,930.66
$230,000	$4,886.82	$3,039.47	$2,471.59	$2,219.55	$2,090.01	$2,018.41
$240,000	$5,099.29	$3,171.62	$2,579.05	$2,316.05	$2,180.88	$2,106.17
$250,000	$5,311.76	$3,303.77	$2,686.51	$2,412.55	$2,271.75	$2,193.93
$260,000	$5,524.23	$3,435.92	$2,793.97	$2,509.06	$2,362.62	$2,281.69
$270,000	$5,736.70	$3,568.07	$2,901.43	$2,605.56	$2,453.49	$2,369.44
$280,000	$5,949.17	$3,700.22	$3,008.89	$2,702.06	$2,544.36	$2,457.20
$290,000	$6,161.64	$3,832.37	$3,116.35	$2,798.56	$2,635.23	$2,544.96
$300,000	$6,374.11	$3,964.52	$3,223.82	$2,895.06	$2,726.10	$2,632.71
$310,000	$6,586.58	$4,096.67	$3,331.28	$2,991.57	$2,816.97	$2,720.47

Interest Rate: 10.50%

Amount Borrowed	Length of Loan (in Years)					
	5	10	15	20	25	30
$50,000	$1,074.70	$674.67	$552.70	$499.19	$472.09	$457.37
$60,000	$1,289.63	$809.61	$663.24	$599.03	$566.51	$548.84
$70,000	$1,504.57	$944.54	$773.78	$698.87	$660.93	$640.32
$80,000	$1,719.51	$1,079.48	$884.32	$798.70	$755.35	$731.79
$90,000	$1,934.45	$1,214.41	$994.86	$898.54	$849.76	$823.27
$100,000	$2,149.39	$1,349.35	$1,105.40	$998.38	$944.18	$914.74
$110,000	$2,364.33	$1,484.28	$1,215.94	$1,098.22	$1,038.60	$1,006.21
$120,000	$2,579.27	$1,619.22	$1,326.48	$1,198.06	$1,133.02	$1,097.69
$130,000	$2,794.21	$1,754.15	$1,437.02	$1,297.89	$1,227.44	$1,189.16
$140,000	$3,009.15	$1,889.09	$1,547.56	$1,397.73	$1,321.85	$1,280.64
$150,000	$3,224.09	$2,024.02	$1,658.10	$1,497.57	$1,416.27	$1,372.11
$160,000	$3,439.02	$2,158.96	$1,768.64	$1,597.41	$1,510.69	$1,463.58
$170,000	$3,653.96	$2,293.89	$1,879.18	$1,697.25	$1,605.11	$1,555.06
$180,000	$3,868.90	$2,428.83	$1,989.72	$1,797.08	$1,699.53	$1,646.53
$190,000	$4,083.84	$2,563.76	$2,100.26	$1,896.92	$1,793.95	$1,738.00
$200,000	$4,298.78	$2,698.70	$2,210.80	$1,996.76	$1,888.36	$1,829.48
$210,000	$4,513.72	$2,833.63	$2,321.34	$2,096.60	$1,982.78	$1,920.95
$220,000	$4,728.66	$2,968.57	$2,431.88	$2,196.44	$2,077.20	$2,012.43
$230,000	$4,943.60	$3,103.50	$2,542.42	$2,296.27	$2,171.62	$2,103.90
$240,000	$5,158.54	$3,238.44	$2,652.96	$2,396.11	$2,266.04	$2,195.37
$250,000	$5,373.48	$3,373.37	$2,763.50	$2,495.95	$2,360.45	$2,286.85
$260,000	$5,588.41	$3,508.31	$2,874.04	$2,595.79	$2,454.87	$2,378.32
$270,000	$5,803.35	$3,643.24	$2,984.58	$2,695.63	$2,549.29	$2,469.80
$280,000	$6,018.29	$3,778.18	$3,095.12	$2,795.46	$2,643.71	$2,561.27
$290,000	$6,233.23	$3,913.11	$3,205.66	$2,895.30	$2,738.13	$2,652.74
$300,000	$6,448.17	$4,048.05	$3,316.20	$2,995.14	$2,832.55	$2,744.22
$310,000	$6,663.11	$4,182.98	$3,426.74	$3,094.98	$2,926.96	$2,835.69

Interest Rate: 11.00%

Amount Borrowed	Length of Loan (in Years)					
	5	10	15	20	25	30
$50,000	$1,087.12	$688.75	$568.30	$516.09	$490.06	$476.16
$60,000	$1,304.55	$826.50	$681.96	$619.31	$588.07	$571.39
$70,000	$1,521.97	$964.25	$795.62	$722.53	$686.08	$666.63
$80,000	$1,739.39	$1,102.00	$909.28	$825.75	$784.09	$761.86
$90,000	$1,956.82	$1,239.75	$1,022.94	$928.97	$882.10	$857.09
$100,000	$2,174.24	$1,377.50	$1,136.60	$1,032.19	$980.11	$952.32
$110,000	$2,391.67	$1,515.25	$1,250.26	$1,135.41	$1,078.12	$1,047.56
$120,000	$2,609.09	$1,653.00	$1,363.92	$1,238.63	$1,176.14	$1,142.79
$130,000	$2,826.51	$1,790.75	$1,477.58	$1,341.84	$1,274.15	$1,238.02
$140,000	$3,043.94	$1,928.50	$1,591.24	$1,445.06	$1,372.16	$1,333.25
$150,000	$3,261.36	$2,066.25	$1,704.90	$1,548.28	$1,470.17	$1,428.49
$160,000	$3,478.79	$2,204.00	$1,818.56	$1,651.50	$1,568.18	$1,523.72
$170,000	$3,696.21	$2,341.75	$1,932.21	$1,754.72	$1,666.19	$1,618.95
$180,000	$3,913.64	$2,479.50	$2,045.87	$1,857.94	$1,764.20	$1,714.18
$190,000	$4,131.06	$2,617.25	$2,159.53	$1,961.16	$1,862.21	$1,809.41
$200,000	$4,348.48	$2,755.00	$2,273.19	$2,064.38	$1,960.23	$1,904.65
$210,000	$4,565.91	$2,892.75	$2,386.85	$2,167.60	$2,058.24	$1,999.88
$220,000	$4,783.33	$3,030.50	$2,500.51	$2,270.81	$2,156.25	$2,095.11
$230,000	$5,000.76	$3,168.25	$2,614.17	$2,374.03	$2,254.26	$2,190.34
$240,000	$5,218.18	$3,306.00	$2,727.83	$2,477.25	$2,352.27	$2,285.58
$250,000	$5,435.61	$3,443.75	$2,841.49	$2,580.47	$2,450.28	$2,380.81
$260,000	$5,653.03	$3,581.50	$2,955.15	$2,683.69	$2,548.29	$2,476.04
$270,000	$5,870.45	$3,719.25	$3,068.81	$2,786.91	$2,646.31	$2,571.27
$280,000	$6,087.88	$3,857.00	$3,182.47	$2,890.13	$2,744.32	$2,666.51
$290,000	$6,305.30	$3,994.75	$3,296.13	$2,993.35	$2,842.33	$2,761.74
$300,000	$6,522.73	$4,132.50	$3,409.79	$3,096.57	$2,940.34	$2,856.97
$310,000	$6,740.15	$4,270.25	$3,523.45	$3,199.78	$3,038.35	$2,952.20

Interest Rate: 11.50%

Amount Borrowed	Length of Loan (in Years)					
	5	10	15	20	25	30
$50,000	$1,099.63	$702.98	$584.09	$533.21	$508.23	$495.15
$60,000	$1,319.56	$843.57	$700.91	$639.86	$609.88	$594.17
$70,000	$1,539.48	$984.17	$817.73	$746.50	$711.53	$693.20
$80,000	$1,759.41	$1,124.76	$934.55	$853.14	$813.18	$792.23
$90,000	$1,979.33	$1,265.36	$1,051.37	$959.79	$914.82	$891.26
$100,000	$2,199.26	$1,405.95	$1,168.19	$1,066.43	$1,016.47	$990.29
$110,000	$2,419.19	$1,546.55	$1,285.01	$1,173.07	$1,118.12	$1,089.32
$120,000	$2,639.11	$1,687.15	$1,401.83	$1,279.72	$1,219.76	$1,188.35
$130,000	$2,859.04	$1,827.74	$1,518.65	$1,386.36	$1,321.41	$1,287.38
$140,000	$3,078.97	$1,968.34	$1,635.47	$1,493.00	$1,423.06	$1,386.41
$150,000	$3,298.89	$2,108.93	$1,752.28	$1,599.64	$1,524.70	$1,485.44
$160,000	$3,518.82	$2,249.53	$1,869.10	$1,706.29	$1,626.35	$1,584.47
$170,000	$3,738.74	$2,390.12	$1,985.92	$1,812.93	$1,728.00	$1,683.50
$180,000	$3,958.67	$2,530.72	$2,102.74	$1,919.57	$1,829.64	$1,782.52
$190,000	$4,178.60	$2,671.31	$2,219.56	$2,026.22	$1,931.29	$1,881.55
$200,000	$4,398.52	$2,811.91	$2,336.38	$2,132.86	$2,032.94	$1,980.58
$210,000	$4,618.45	$2,952.50	$2,453.20	$2,239.50	$2,134.58	$2,079.61
$220,000	$4,838.37	$3,093.10	$2,570.02	$2,346.15	$2,236.23	$2,178.64
$230,000	$5,058.30	$3,233.70	$2,686.84	$2,452.79	$2,337.88	$2,277.67
$240,000	$5,278.23	$3,374.29	$2,803.66	$2,559.43	$2,439.53	$2,376.70
$250,000	$5,498.15	$3,514.89	$2,920.47	$2,666.07	$2,541.17	$2,475.73
$260,000	$5,718.08	$3,655.48	$3,037.29	$2,772.72	$2,642.82	$2,574.76
$270,000	$5,938.00	$3,796.08	$3,154.11	$2,879.36	$2,744.47	$2,673.79
$280,000	$6,157.93	$3,936.67	$3,270.93	$2,986.00	$2,846.11	$2,772.82
$290,000	$6,377.86	$4,077.27	$3,387.75	$3,092.65	$2,947.76	$2,871.85
$300,000	$6,597.78	$4,217.86	$3,504.57	$3,199.29	$3,049.41	$2,970.87
$310,000	$6,817.71	$4,358.46	$3,621.39	$3,305.93	$3,151.05	$3,069.90

Interest Rate: 12.00%

Amount Borrowed	Length of Loan (in Years)					
	5	10	15	20	25	30
$50,000	$1,112.22	$717.35	$600.08	$550.54	$526.61	$514.31
$60,000	$1,334.67	$860.83	$720.10	$660.65	$631.93	$617.17
$70,000	$1,557.11	$1,004.30	$840.12	$770.76	$737.26	$720.03
$80,000	$1,779.56	$1,147.77	$960.13	$880.87	$842.58	$822.89
$90,000	$2,002.00	$1,291.24	$1,080.15	$990.98	$947.90	$925.75
$100,000	$2,224.44	$1,434.71	$1,200.17	$1,101.09	$1,053.22	$1,028.61
$110,000	$2,446.89	$1,578.18	$1,320.18	$1,211.19	$1,158.55	$1,131.47
$120,000	$2,669.33	$1,721.65	$1,440.20	$1,321.30	$1,263.87	$1,234.34
$130,000	$2,891.78	$1,865.12	$1,560.22	$1,431.41	$1,369.19	$1,337.20
$140,000	$3,114.22	$2,008.59	$1,680.24	$1,541.52	$1,474.51	$1,440.06
$150,000	$3,336.67	$2,152.06	$1,800.25	$1,651.63	$1,579.84	$1,542.92
$160,000	$3,559.11	$2,295.54	$1,920.27	$1,761.74	$1,685.16	$1,645.78
$170,000	$3,781.56	$2,439.01	$2,040.29	$1,871.85	$1,790.48	$1,748.64
$180,000	$4,004.00	$2,582.48	$2,160.30	$1,981.96	$1,895.80	$1,851.50
$190,000	$4,226.45	$2,725.95	$2,280.32	$2,092.06	$2,001.13	$1,954.36
$200,000	$4,448.89	$2,869.42	$2,400.34	$2,202.17	$2,106.45	$2,057.23
$210,000	$4,671.33	$3,012.89	$2,520.35	$2,312.28	$2,211.77	$2,160.09
$220,000	$4,893.78	$3,156.36	$2,640.37	$2,422.39	$2,317.09	$2,262.95
$230,000	$5,116.22	$3,299.83	$2,760.39	$2,532.50	$2,422.42	$2,365.81
$240,000	$5,338.67	$3,443.30	$2,880.40	$2,642.61	$2,527.74	$2,468.67
$250,000	$5,561.11	$3,586.77	$3,000.42	$2,752.72	$2,633.06	$2,571.53
$260,000	$5,783.56	$3,730.24	$3,120.44	$2,862.82	$2,738.38	$2,674.39
$270,000	$6,006.00	$3,873.72	$3,240.45	$2,972.93	$2,843.71	$2,777.25
$280,000	$6,228.45	$4,017.19	$3,360.47	$3,083.04	$2,949.03	$2,880.12
$290,000	$6,450.89	$4,160.66	$3,480.49	$3,193.15	$3,054.35	$2,982.98
$300,000	$6,673.33	$4,304.13	$3,600.50	$3,303.26	$3,159.67	$3,085.84
$310,000	$6,895.78	$4,447.60	$3,720.52	$3,413.37	$3,264.99	$3,188.70

index

about the authors

Donna Raskin is the author of *Yoga Beats the Blues* and *The Buddha: His Life and Teachings* (Fair Winds Press) as well as books for Rodale Press. She has contributed articles to *Yoga Journal, Prevention, Fit, American Health, Fit/Yoga, Ms., Self, Shape,* and *Cooking Light*. Donna has lived in six states, but currently she and her son view the ocean from their house in Rockport, Massachusetts.

Susan Hawthorne has enjoyed over twenty-three years in the real estate business in downtown Boston, offering professional service and advice as an agent, friend, negotiator, babysitter, personal shopper, and arbitrator—which is all part of the real estate profession. Prior to opening her own business with a partner and purchasing a RE/MAX franchise, Susan worked in several real estate companies. Before her real estate career, Susan worked in advertising in Connecticut and Boston. Susan was raised in New York, is married, has one son and two stepchildren. She has one grandchild and is looking forward to semi-retirement.